PRINCETON SERMONS

OTHER SOLID GROUND TITLES

We recently celebrated our eighth anniversary of uncovering buried treasure to the glory of God. During these eight years we have produced over 225 volumes. A sample is listed below:

Biblical & Theological Studies: *Addresses to Commemorate the 100th Anniversary of Princeton Theological Seminary in 1912* by Allis, Machen, Wilson, Vos, Warfield and many more.
Power of the Pulpit by Gardiner Spring
Thoughts on Preaching by James W. Alexander
Notes on Galatians by J. Gresham Machen
The Origin of Paul's Religion by J. Gresham Machen
A Scientific Investigation of the Old Testament by R.D. Wilson
Theology on Fire: *Sermons from Joseph A. Alexander*
Evangelical Truth: *Sermons for the Family* by Archibald Alexander
A Shepherd's Heart: *Pastoral Sermons of James W. Alexander*
Grace & Glory: *Sermons from Princeton Chapel* by Geerhardus Vos
The Lord of Glory by Benjamin B. Warfield
The Person & Work of the Holy Spirit by Benjamin B. Warfield
The Power of God unto Salvation by Benjamin B. Warfield
Calvin Memorial Addresses by Warfield, Johnson, Orr, Webb...
The Five Points of Calvinism by Robert Lewis Dabney
Annals of the American Presbyterian Pulpit by W.B. Sprague
The Word & Prayer: *Classic Devotions from the Pen of John Calvin*
A Body of Divinity: *Sum and Substance of Christian Doctrine* by Ussher
The Complete Works of Thomas Manton (in 22 volumes)
A Puritan New Testament Commentary by John Trapp
Exposition of the Epistle to the Hebrews by William Gouge
Exposition of the Epistle of Jude by William Jenkyn
Lectures on the Book of Esther by Thomas M'Crie
Lectures on the Book of Acts by John Dick

To order any of our titles please contact us in one of three ways:

Call us at **1-866-789-7423**
Email us at **sgcb@charter.net**
Visit our website at **www.solid-ground-books.com**

PRINCETON SERMONS

CHAPEL ADDRESSES
FROM 1891-1892

JAMES A. AIKEN
JOHN D. DAVIS
WILLIAM H. GREEN
CASPAR W. HODGE
JAMES O. MURRAY
FRANCIS L. PATTON
WILLIAM M. PAXTON
BENJAMIN B. WARFIELD

SOLID GROUND CHRISTIAN BOOKS
BIRMINGHAM, ALABAMA USA

Solid Ground Christian Books
PO Box 660132
Vestavia Hills AL 35266
205-443-0311
sgcb@charter.net
solid-ground-books.com

Princeton Sermons
Chapel Addresses from 1891-1892
by James A. Aiken
John D. Davis
William H. Green
Caspar W. Hodge
James O. Murray
Francis L. Patton
William M. Paxton
Benjamin B. Warfield

First published in 1892 by Fleming H. Revell Co.
First Solid Ground edition September 2009

COVER IMAGE: This is a photograph of the faculty of Princeton Seminary in 1891-1892, and used with permission from the Princeton Seminary Library in Princeton, NJ.

Cover design by Borgo Design, Tuscaloosa, AL

ISBN: 978-159925-2193

PREFACE.

THE sermons printed in this volume were not written for publication. They represent the ordinary sermons preached Sabbath by Sabbath in the chapel of the Theological Seminary at Princeton. The most of them were preached during the term of last year (1891-92). The exceptions to this are chiefly due to the desire to include in the volume sermons of two of the professors in the seminary who were taken from it during the first half of that term—the late Drs. C. W. Hodge and C. A. Aiken. The volume is greatly enriched, and at the same time a truer conspectus is given of the year's preaching in the chapel, by the inclusion in it also of sermons by two of the officers of the seminary who are as closely identified with it as the professors themselves, and who frequently grace its pulpit—President Patton and Dean Murray of the college. The sermons of President Patton here printed are distinctly college sermons, and belong to the opening and close of the college year. Dean Murray's were preached in the seminary chapel.

The fact that these sermons are addressed to

an audience composed almost entirely of divinity students has no doubt given them a special character. Among other things it has brought it about that they are, as a class, rather didactic than evangelizing sermons. If on one side this may be a weakness, possibly on another it may be not altogether without some advantage. There is good reason, at any rate, to hope that a body of sermons addressed to a distinctively Christian audience may not be without general usefulness. A thoughtful passage from a recent work by Prof. William Milligan, D.D., of the University of Aberdeen ("The Ascension and Heavenly Priesthood of our Lord," p. 281), may be quoted here in support of such a hope. In justice to Dr. Milligan it must be remembered that in the immediate vicinity of this passage he fully recognizes the importance and duty of evangelizing preaching. Bearing this in mind, the following remarks will doubtless be instructive:

"Important as the sacred writers knew their message to the world to be, they never fail to exhibit the conviction that it was even more important to the churches; that, while they had no doubt to convert unbelievers, it was still more imperatively required that they should edify believers and carry them on unto perfection; and that the different members of the Body needed to be compacted into one, each working well in its own place, and all working smoothly together, before the Church could successfully accomplish her mission.

Hence the exhortations to growth in every Christian grace with which the New Testament Epistles abound; hence the joy of thankfulness with which every manifestation of that growth was hailed by the Apostles and apostolic men who wrote them; hence the prominence continually assigned to that order of things which, embodying the precept of our Lord, first makes the tree good that its fruit may be good also; and hence, to take only one noteworthy example from the writings of St. Paul, when that Apostle tells us of the object which the ascended Lord had in view by the gift of his various ministries, the conversion of the world is not mentioned. Everything has relation to the Church. Apostles, prophets, evangelists, pastors, and teachers are given 'for the perfecting of the saints, unto the work of ministering, unto the building up of the body of Christ; till we all attain unto the unity of the faith, and of the knowledge of the Son of God, unto a full-grown man, unto the measure of the stature of the fullness of Christ, . . . from whom all the body fitly framed and knit together, . . . maketh the increase of the body unto the building up of itself in love.'"

On some such ground as this, it may be hoped that these sermons may be useful in much broader circles than that for which they were originally prepared, and to which they were in the first instance preached.

CONTENTS.

	PAGE
CHRIST'S DESIRE FOR HIS PEOPLE (John 17:24)......	1

    By Prof. WILLIAM HENRY GREEN, D.D., LL.D.

THE PROMISE OF THE SPIRIT (John 16:12–15)........ 29
    By the late Prof. CASPAR WISTAR HODGE, D.D., LL.D.

VALIANT FOR THE TRUTH (Jeremiah 9:3)............ 50
    By the late Prof. CHARLES A. AIKEN, Ph.D., D.D.

SALVATION AS A WORK (Philippians 1:6)............ 75
    By Prof. WILLIAM M. PAXTON, D.D., LL.D.

INCARNATE TRUTH (John 1:14)...................... 94
    By Prof. BENJAMIN B. WARFIELD, D.D., LL.D.

FIRST INTERVIEW WITH THE CHRIST (John 1:37–42).. 115
    By Prof. JOHN D. DAVIS, Ph.D.

RELIGION IN COLLEGE (1 John 2:13)................. 130
    By President FRANCIS L. PATTON, D.D., LL.D.

THE LETTER AND THE SPIRIT (2 Cor. 3:6)........... 159
    By President FRANCIS L. PATTON, D.D., LL.D.

CHRIST AS A MAN OF PRAYER (Luke 6:12)........... 192
    By Prof. JAMES O. MURRAY, D.D., LL.D.

CONTENTS.

	PAGE
THE TRANSFIGURATION OF LIFE BY CHRIST (Luke 9:29).	212

    By Prof. JAMES O. MURRAY, D.D., LL.D.

CHRISTIAN MANLINESS (1 Cor. 16:13) 235

    By Prof. WILLIAM HENRY GREEN, D.D., LL.D.

THE POWER OF CHRIST'S RESURRECTION (Phil. 3:10)... 260

    By the late Prof. CASPAR WISTAR HODGE, D.D., LL.D.

DRIFTING (Hebrews 2:1)........................... 278

    By the late Prof. CHARLES A. AIKEN, Ph.D., D.D.

HOW WE SPEND OUR YEARS (Psalms 90:9)........... 298

    By Prof. WILLIAM M. PAXTON, D.D., LL.D.

THE CHRISTIAN'S ATTITUDE TOWARD DEATH (2 Cor. 5:1-10) 316

    By Prof. BENJAMIN B. WARFIELD, DD., LL.D.

THE VISION OF THE KING IN HIS HOLINESS (Isaiah 6:5-7) 338

    By Prof. JOHN D. DAVIS, Ph.D.

CHRIST'S DESIRE FOR HIS PEOPLE.

By Prof. William Henry Green, D.D., LL.D.

"Father, I will that they also, whom thou hast given me, be with me where I am; that they may behold my glory, which thou hast given me."—John 17:24.

IF our minds were in perfect harmony with the mind of Christ our views would in many respects be greatly altered. Many things that we now desire and long for would lose much of their attractiveness; and other things that we dread and shrink from would cease to be unwelcome.

The great Redeemer is in this chapter giving utterance to the desires of his heart on behalf of his people. And the closing petition, the crowning one of all, is that they might be with him to behold his glory. He had been with them here in his humiliation and life of toilsome sorrow. But the termination of his work on earth was now rapidly approaching, and he was shortly to leave the world and enter into his glory. The anticipated departure of their Lord, whom they loved and upon whom they leaned for more, far more, than any merely human friend or teacher could have brought them, had filled their hearts with sadness and grief. How lonely, cheerless, helpless would they be in this world if Jesus were taken away from them! But the separation, which grieved them so much, shall not last forever. It is his will that they should be with him where he is. The last and highest blessing that he solicits for them is their removal from earth to heaven.

This is desirable in the first place that they may be delivered from the contact and contamination of evil. He had before prayed that while they were in the world they might be kept from the evil which so abounds in it. It is a priceless benefit to have a divine shield interposed between us and all surrounding dangers; to be enabled to walk dryshod through the very midst of the tempestuous sea, and while the waves thereof roar and are troubled, and its billows threaten to ingulf us, to find that they are held back by an almighty arm and a pathway cloven before us, so that we can pass unharmed along our perilous way. It is an inestimable blessing to have divine guidance and heavenly supplies in the desert, the cloud and the fire going before us in the trackless waste; and while on every hand nothing appears but barren and arid sands, in the midst of which it seems as though we must certainly famish and perish from thirst, to find that the clouds are bidden to rain down food upon us day by day and the rock to pour forth its cooling streams. But the beneficence is more complete which not merely guards and protects in the midst of evils, but dissipates and removes the evils themselves; which brings the people safely to the shore beyond the reach of the angry waves of the sea; and which leads them out of the waste and howling wilderness and fixes their secure abode in the land flowing with milk and honey.

This is a world of evil, and evil is inseparably connected with every condition here. Blessed be God, it is not a world of unmingled evil. There is much in it to be grateful for; much that is good and holy and pure; much that turns our thoughts to God; much that is adapted to help us upward toward him and to quicken and stimulate us in his service. There is the converse and companionship of the good. There are those among us who deserve to be styled the excellent of the earth, whose spirit is pure and Christ-like, whose conversation is in heaven, who breathe a heavenly atmosphere, and their faces are radiant from their devout and holy intercourse with God. We find it not only delightful and refreshing, but elevating and ennobling, to come into contact with them. We cannot be with them without being sensibly warmed by the glow of holy affections which burns in their bosoms, without having a livelier interest awakened within us in the things of God. We come forth from their society and find that the objects of faith have assumed a more practical reality to us; our convictions are freshened and deepened that the matters of eternity are really the great concern; and we have gathered new inward resolves that they shall henceforth supremely engage our thoughts and our activities. But we return to the companionship of ordinary men more on a level with ourselves, and we resemble a solitary coal drawn forth from among blazing embers and laid amidst lumps of ice, where it is speedily blackened and chilled. We relapse again into our customary state. We fall to the condition of those around us, above which our poor, weak aspirations are insufficient to raise us. The most of those around us are absorbed with the world—busily, eagerly pressing their earthly schemes, occupied with earthly cares, engaged in earthly pursuits, reveling in earthly pleasures, extolling the worth of earthly things, living as though this world were all. And they who have the love of God in their hearts hide it so far out of sight that we often scarcely feel the difference between them and others. And thus our friends, our associates, the companions of our daily life, go rushing on in the same heedless chase of earthly vanities, and we speed on with the multitude, unable to breast the current or to resist the accumulated pressure which sweeps us along with those who surround us.

Oh, to be lifted out of this fatal whirl, to be where we should be buoyed up and helped onward instead of being drawn downward by those who are about us! If those choice spirits who are so helpful to us could be with us always, ever lending us their aid, and theirs the only influences to which we were subjected! If we could be in a community made up of the good alone, where the love of Christ reigned in every heart and all were possessed of his pure and blessed Spirit, so that from the whole circle of our companionship should come only influences that were quickening, elevating, and purifying!

But such a community is not to be found in this world, which is one of mingled good and evil, and where too often the bad predominates. It is only in the heavenly glory that a society of unmixed good is realized. Into that world nothing defiled or that defileth shall ever enter; the companionship is with angels and the glorified spirits of the just; all that pass thither from this world have washed their robes, and made them white in the blood of the Lamb, and all their weaknesses and imperfections have been removed. There all lips are vocal with the praises of Him who sits upon the throne, and of the Lamb; every heart is responsive to each utterance of the divine will; every breast swells with thankfulness and joyful gratitude for all the blessings of redeeming love; the image of Christ is reflected in every form; untarnished excellence radiates from all. How is it possible to move in such society as this without being borne aloft by the spirit which pervades the whole, without being ourselves absorbed in that one supreme, controlling object of interest which dwells in every heart, without kindling into admiration of that one theme which glows on every tongue, without gazing with fond delight upon that one center of attraction to which all eyes are turned, without sharing in the love and purity and holiness which everywhere prevail? There are the angels who shouted over the new-born creation and who have watched with growing wonder and delight the developments of God's plan of grace from that day to this; whose voices blended in that sweet chorus heard by the shepherds of Bethlehem when the Lord of glory was born a babe; who gazed with indescribable amazement upon the astonishing scenes of Gethsemane and of Calvary; who saw the Son of God, when his humiliation was ended, reascend the skies and amid the acclamations of the entire heavenly host assume his seat on the right hand of God; and who have since gone forth with willing feet on numberless ministries of love to the heirs of salvation. There are the patriarchs, who have found the city of foundations for which they once looked and longed. There are the prophets, who eagerly watched for the coming dawn before the day had broken, and who foretold its future brightness. There are the apostles, who companied with Jesus in the days of his flesh. There is the noble army of martyrs, who suffered the loss of all things and gave up life itself for the love they bore his name. There is the entire array of those of every age, and out of every clime and nation, who have lived the life of faith and gotten the victory over sin and corruption; the real heroes, the true nobility of earth, living and dying in obscurity and poverty it may be, hidden from the sight of men, despised, maligned, suffering obloquy and reproach, of whom the world was not worthy, their names emblazoned on no scroll of fame, yet held in honor there and written in the Lamb's book of life. There, too, are our own kindred and friends who have departed in the faith and hope of the Gospel, not as we knew them here in the feebleness of mortal clay, but transfigured and transformed, made equal unto the angels, made like to the Son of God himself. What a goodly assemblage is this, what a world to be introduced into! What invigoration to every holy principle, what stimulus to every right affection, what enlargement of soul, what confirmation in all that is right and good! What pulses of heavenly life would grow out of the very contact with the heavenly world! So that we can here see one reason why the loving Redeemer did not end his supplications when he had prayed that his people should be kept from the evil that is in the world; but he likewise adds, "Father, I will that they also, whom thou hast given me, be with me where I am."

And then the world itself, in which we live, hampers and restrains us. All that we are conversant with here, our occupations, pleasures, possessions, bind our hearts to earth and hold us back from God. The visible, tangible, and outward obtrudes itself upon us at every turn. We are surrounded on every hand and at all times by sensible things; they force themselves upon our attention, they engage our thoughts. The necessities of our daily existence compel us to be largely occupied with them. What shall we eat, what shall we drink, wherewithal shall we be clothed? are questions that are daily recurring and cannot be pushed altogether aside. But the spiritual, the heavenly, and the divine are out of sight and beyond the reach of any of our senses. It is only by faith that we are assured of them. It requires an effort to bring them before our minds, and constantly repeated efforts to keep them there. The clamor and din of worldliness so stun our ears that we fail to hear the appeals that God and eternity and salvation are making to us. And as the hand held near the eyes will shut out from sight the immense globe of the sun, so do the temporal and the fleeting and the unsubstantial things of earth, by sheer proximity, to a great extent exclude from our thoughts and our affections things that are eternal and unchanging, the true, enduring realities. We are fettered by sense, and we can no more emancipate ourselves from these bonds than we can rid ourselves of the law of gravitation and soar upward to the stars.

We are not, indeed, left wholly without help in this matter. We have the Word of God, revealing things to us in their just proportions, recording the unerring judgments of the Most High regarding earth and heaven, things present and things to come. We have the sacred ordinances and means of grace, which are channels of divine influence upon our souls. We have our Sabbaths and seasons of devotion, when divine things do or should wholly engage our thoughts and are brought near to us; when the world, its scenes and cares, are shut out, and God and Christ and salvation occupy our minds. Nevertheless we are at an immense disadvantage all the while. We know that the earth is as a point compared with the vastly greater magnitude of the fixed stars that stud the nightly heavens. Yet, in spite of all that we know and believe, we cannot alter the fact that they do appear differently to outward sense. The world seems to be of enormous size, and the star but a twinkling, inconsiderable point. But if our position were changed, how would everything alter and adjust itself at once! If instead of standing on the earth we were transported to the star, that twinkling point would become the boundless globe, and this tiny earth would vanish out of sight.

It is possible, indeed, by divine grace to live even in this cold and frozen region. God can and does preserve his children from the evil that is in the world. There is a stunted vegetation in the midst of polar snows which continues to exist even in those dreary desolations, checked and benumbed in the long night and dreadful winter, but never wholly extinguished; so that when the sun returns —though his rays fall aslant and are shorn of much of their fervor—and the frozen ground is slightly thawed at the surface, these little plants peep up in their brief summer and put forth their tiny leaves and open their little buds, in a manner at once surprising and beautiful to behold. Yes, the abounding goodness of God has produced and maintains life even there, though all about is so deadening and uncongenial. And there are graceful forms of beauty to admire, and lovely tints and handiwork that speaks of the skill of the great Artist. The adventurous voyager who has pushed his bark amid the perils of the icy sea to that remote inhospitable region beholds them with astonishment. Yet they are weak and puny after all. They cannot be otherwise, from the conditions of their growth. The marvel is that they can exist at all. What are they in comparison with the size and beauty and endless variety, and rich, bewildering profusion and boundless range of tropical vegetation, where the fertile earth, warmed by the constant rays of the vertical sun, sends up its teeming products, covering continents with giant forests and a limitless expanse of verdure, gorgeously arrayed with painted bloom, grass, shrubs, and trees crowding every inch of space, decked with gay flowers of every brilliant hue, boughs bending beneath their burden of luscious fruits, the air filled with agreeable perfumes, and the odor of sweet spices wafted from every side. Shall not the great Husbandman transplant what with immense care he has been nurturing here amid chilling blasts and inhospitable winters into the paradise prepared for them above, where "everlasting spring abides and never-withering flowers"? Into what new and vigorous life shall they not develop, what unexpected beauty shall they not unfold, what noble growths shall arise out of these sparse and stunted forms!

It is possible to maintain the life of God in this unfriendly world, though at this vast distance from our Father's house, the great realities removed from sight, and everything about us tending to draw us away from our true end. It is nevertheless possible to learn to see God in everything and to serve God in all we do, whether we eat or drink, still glorifying him; to live near to God at all times, to walk with him in all the concerns of every day as a man walketh with his friend, to grasp the eternal substance to the disregard of the fleeting shadows, even though these latter press themselves upon every sense and the former can only be attained to by an earnest struggle. It is possible by the grace of God to lead a life of faith, to walk by faith and not by outward sense; to resist the temptations to worldliness and self-indulgence and self-seeking which grow out of every circumstance of our situation, out of our necessary occupations, and out of our most innocent pleasures; to hold out even against the solicitations of our great adversary, which beset us on every side, and the snares with which he would entangle us to our ruin. And what is the hardest of all, it is possible to maintain a successful fight against one's own inward corruptions. For we have to contend not only against the world and Satan, but against our own evil propensities and passions, against the law of sin which is in our members, the flesh lusting against the spirit, and the spirit struggling against the flesh; ourselves at war against ourselves, treachery within leagued with foes without, so that we cannot be sure even of ourselves, and dare not trust ourselves. Our most dangerous enemies are, in fact, within.

And yet in spite of all and through all God's children may be kept, and are kept. God giveth them the victory. But it is at the price of incessant vigilance. It is by a perpetual struggle, and they carry on their warfare at fearful odds. They may be thankful if they come off with their lives from the desperate encounter. They cannot well avoid being scarred and wounded in the fight; and they will be obliged to drag themselves along in their forced marches, faint with fatigue and loss of blood, dispirited sometimes and almost disheartened, as though the war would never end. But it shall end, and end gloriously, too. Oh, what loud ringing cheers go up from the lips of the veteran soldier as he catches sight of the flag of victory, and sees the signal displayed which tells him that the ranks of the foe have everywhere given way in disordered rout! The field is won. The victory is assured. The weary campaign is over.

Friends gather tearful around the pallid corpse —the face in meek repose, the eyes closed, never to weep again, the bosom still, never to heave another sigh. But the glad spirit, which has taken its upward flight from that wasted form, is already singing its new-born song of thanksgiving and triumph before the throne, and rejoicing in the fulfillment of the Saviour's prayer, "Father, I will that they also, whom thou hast given me, be with me where I am."

This prayer of Jesus looks, as we have now seen, to the deliverance of his people from a world of sin. It has another negative feature of great preciousness at which we must also glance before we can proceed to consider the positive blessings which it contemplates. This is also a world of suffering and sorrow; and when the Saviour prays that they whom the Father has given him may be with him where he is, he prays that they may be released from all the suffering and the sorrow that the world contains.

Not but there is much here to be thankful for, much true happiness, much to enjoy, many prolific springs of satisfaction and delight. This world has with the most benevolent regard to the wants of our nature been adapted to minister to our gratification. Every sense is an inlet of pleasure, and the objects are numberless from which this pleasure may be derived. Light is sweet to the eyes. The ear is charmed with melody of sound. Food has a relish, which delights our taste. Our intellectual nature is aroused and pleasurably excited by the multitudinous objects of knowledge, which excite our interest and stimulate inquiries that are their own reward. Our social nature finds satisfaction in the company of friends and solace in all that is engaging and delightful in domestic life. And for our spiritual nature there is graciously provided the joy of salvation, the joy of pardoned sin, the joy of holy intercourse with God and communion with his saints, the joy of the Holy Ghost, which passes through every gradation from calm and peaceful frames to raptures that are unspeakable and full of glory. There are numerous sources of rich enjoyment in this world which it would argue criminal ingratitude to overlook or to depreciate. There are fountains of elevated and rational gratification at which we may drink and drink again. He who has a thankful heart for God's mercies will always find mercies in his lot to be thankful for.

And yet we cannot annul the fact that God has cursed the ground on which we tread for the sins of men. It brings forth thorns and thistles, and man must wring his bread from it by the sweat of his brow. He is born to trouble, and this is a heritage from which he cannot escape. He who expects perfect and unalloyed satisfaction here expects what never can be found. The same sensitive organization which renders us susceptible to pleasure exposes us likewise to pain. Every possibility of gratification involves a corresponding liability to suffering. Every added possession is a new liability to loss. Each glad anticipation shows us capable of its reverse, the poignancy of disappointment or the heartsickness of hope deferred. He who can smile can weep. Joys that bloom may wither on the stem, and the bright morning may be overcast with clouds. What anxieties gather around every valued treasure! Oh, the distressing instability of earthly good! How it casts its baleful shadow over every scene of present enjoyment! Who knows what shall be on the morrow? Riches take to themselves wings and fly away. Friends that gather around us like the birds of spring may also, like birds of passage, take their flight. And the nearest, dearest group of all, the precious domestic circle—ah! each beloved form only presages the anguish of an additional parting that sooner or later must take place.

From this instability of earthly good, and exposure to privation and suffering, the people of God have no exemption. They have the same liabilities to pains and losses and griefs as other men. They have their full share of trials and afflictions. They are, in fact, characteristically, as a class, the afflicted and the sufferers. The petition of their Lord that they should be kept from the evil that is in the world does not screen them from outward troubles. On the contrary, our heavenly Father uses trouble and affliction as chastisements for their good; though for the present not joyous but grievous, they work out the peaceable fruits of righteousness. Through much tribulation it is ordained that they should enter into the kingdom of heaven. "Whom the Lord loveth he chasteneth, and scourgeth every son whom he receiveth." This is designed to promote their highest welfare by the infinite love and grace of him who doeth all things well. But the bitter is still bitter; and it makes us shudder as we swallow it, though we know there is healing in the draught. And the sorrows of God's children are no less keenly felt because they have learned submission to the divine will and reverently kiss the rod. The very tenderness of their heart makes them, in fact, more sensitive to the stroke; and it adds a new element of poignancy to their grief that *his* hand of love should have found it necessary to afflict them.

And then there is, besides, a large class of painful experiences which are peculiar to pious souls. There are inward griefs and apprehensions, and distressing doubts and fears, and painful struggles and mortifications, and penitent tears and bitter regrets over spiritual delinquencies, and periods of depression and darkness from the hiding of the Lord's face, and the lack of that sense of his favor which is essential to their inward peace. These are trials that the world knows nothing of, and yet which sometimes force from the wrestling, struggling child of God deep-drawn sighs and the half-desponding exclamation, "Who shall deliver me from the body of this death? When will the day dawn and the shadows flee away?"

CHRIST'S DESIRE FOR HIS PEOPLE.

Oh, what a blissful sense of rest shall possess the ransomed soul when this wearisome round of suffering is at an end—when the wandering exile has at last reached his Father's house, and the sorrowing child of God has found repose upon his Saviour's breast; the toils of life all ended, its burdens all laid down, the inward tumult stilled. Henceforth he shall have no more experience of pain or grief or woe, no aching brow, no fevered pulse, no wearied limbs, no load of care; beyond all reach of harm, safe from every foe, forever safe in heaven.

But I must not dwell here: I hasten to remark that the petition of our Lord reaches far beyond all that we have yet considered. Deliverance from this world of sin and suffering is but a preliminary implication in this comprehensive prayer. It is but the necessary antecedent to the blessedness which he supplicates for his people, not that blessedness itself. He prays that they may be with him and behold his glory. To be absent from the body is to be present with the Lord. To depart and be with Christ, says the Apostle, is far better. To be with Christ, whom, having not seen, we love; and in whom, though now we see him not, yet believing, we rejoice with joy unspeakable and full of glory. What rapture in the thought of beholding the face of our Redeemer and our Lord, who from love to us forsook the glories of heaven to suffer and die for our salvation; to see the very head that was crowned with thorns, the hands that were pierced with nails, the face that sweat great drops of blood in the agony of the garden, the lips from which issued such words of grace and tenderness and compassion! To see Jesus, who snatched us from perdition by the sacrifice of himself; to whom we have clung by eager faith as our only hope for pardon and peace with God and everlasting life; that gracious Saviour, who has been our all-in-all, who has spoken peace to our troubled souls and whispered to our contrite hearts, "Thy sins be forgiven thee"; who has borne with us in our weakness and our waywardness; who has cheered us in our hours of despondency and gloom; who has sustained and helped us by his grace and led us all along our course, and guarded and sheltered us and given us the victory, and shed his love abroad in our hearts, and purged us from our sins and delivered us out of all our fears, and prepared a mansion for us in his own blessed abode, and opened heaven for us and brought us safely there to be with him forever. Oh, with what bursting gratitude and joy and love will the ransomed soul gaze and gaze forever, unwearied, on the sacred form of him who loved us and washed us from our sins in his own blood, while his adoring amazement, glad surprise, and admiring, thankful love swell beyond all bounds. What higher idea can we have of supreme felicity than to be with Jesus where he is?

But the petition of the text proceeds "that they may behold my glory which thou hast given me." The glory of the uncreated Son of God—what a transcendent vision must that be! It was a distinguished privilege to see the Son of God in human form in his lowly humiliation. The apostle John, who saw this form once lit up by the momentary radiance of the transfiguration, and who throughout his earthly ministry had seen the manifestations of heavenly love and grace daily beaming forth from the person of Jesus, writes of what was thus displayed on earth before his own eyes, "We have seen his glory, as of the only begotten of the Father." And our Lord said to his disciples that companied with him during his abode on earth, "Blessed are the eyes which see the things that ye see: for I tell you, that many prophets and kings have desired to see those things which ye see, and have not seen them." To see the Son of God even when he walked in Judea and in Galilee in the form of a servant, and to feel that the man before us is really the incarnate God; to see tokens of a power resident in him to which all nature yielded prompt obedience; to see the tempest hushed and the raging waves subside at his command; to hear that voice which opened the eyes of the blind and gave hearing to the deaf and life to the dead, and with divine authority could say to a weeping sinner, "Thy sins are forgiven thee"; to have him tell us of heavenly things who has been himself in heaven, and testifies what he has seen, and tell us of God, who had been with God from eternity, and was God; to behold him who is the very image of the invisible God, to observe the perfections of the Godhead mirrored in his life and coming forth in all his acts—what awe would possess our souls as we reverently gazed upon the form of God manifest in the flesh! And what an unspeakable privilege it would be to be permitted to feel in our own souls the power of that presence, and to place ourselves beneath the molding, quickening, saving energy which emanated from him. What a companionship would this be, beyond all parallel of privilege or blessing on earth! Such honor was granted to the early disciples of our Lord. But no mortal eye was ever permitted to behold his unveiled glory.

Earth has its brilliant spectacles, its grand and showy pageants, such as the splendors of a coronation, when the resources of an empire are summoned to add magnificence to royalty. The monarch all ablaze with jewels and regal decoration; his attendant guards and princely retinue with brilliant and varied uniforms and streaming banners, with martial music moving in stately procession amid chiming bells and peals of artillery and surging masses wild with enthusiasm and rending the air with loud acclaim; the spacious and venerable halls proudly adorned; the imposing ceremonies, the insignia of royalty displayed, the crown and the scepter committed to him who holds them by hereditary right from a long line of kings traced back to remote antiquity, and representative of an acknowledged sway over widespread dominions and millions of loyal population—all this is grandly impressive.

But what is all the pomp and majestic greatness of earth to the splendors which surround the monarch of the skies? The brilliancy, which is feebly represented by the sun shining in its strength; the great white throne, and from the face of him that sits on it the earth and heavens flee away; the surrounding multitudes of the heavenly host, angels that excel in strength, celestial principalities and powers; thousand thousands minister unto him, and ten thousand times ten thousand stand before him, the King of kings and Lord of lords, the ancient of days, his kingdom an everlasting kingdom, his word a word of omnipotence, his scepter swaying the universe; himself adored and worshiped and praised by countless multitudes of glorious and holy creatures, who ascribe to him without ceasing blessing and honor and glory and power.

Oh, the unimagined magnificence of the scene that opens to the gaze of him in whom the petition is fulfilled, "Father, I will that they also, whom thou hast given me, be with me where I am, that they may behold my glory."

And while the soul of the glorified saint is ravished by the sight of these divine splendors, it is chiefly the thought that this exalted glory is the glory of Jesus which transports him with the most supreme delight. The Saviour whom he has feebly tried to love, whom in his feeble measure he has sought to glorify, and in whose spreading kingdom here on earth he has found his liveliest satisfaction, is praised as he cannot praise him. How it rejoices him to see in place of the poor, unworthy tribute rendered to Jesus on the earth, the exalted homage of the skies; to see that Jesus is praised and adored by multitudes on multitudes, who honor him as he deserves to be honored and adored; to see that if the earth is slack in rendering him homage, all heaven is vocal with his praise; that such glory has been given him by his Father as is commensurate with the greatness of his redeeming work; and that notwithstanding the poor, unworthy return which is all that he can render to this adorable and gracious Saviour, he has received an adequate reward for all his love and all his pains in the exaltation and glory which have in consequence been bestowed upon him. And if the ransomed soul, transported with the spectacle of his Redeemer's glory, can do no more, he can at least with a rejoicing heart add one more voice to the universal chorus, "Worthy is the Lamb that was slain to receive power, and riches, and wisdom, and strength, and honor, and glory, and blessing."

But the rapture of gazing is not all that is linked with beholding the glory of Christ. How can one stand in the sunshine and not be illuminated, or approach the fire and not be warmed, or be set in constant contact with the beautiful and the true and not be instructed and refined? The glory of Christ is not a mere spectacle to be passively beheld, but a power ever radiating forth upon those who gaze upon it. It not only entrances with delight, it is transforming. Life, holiness, salvation, stream forth from him who is the fountain of life and healing. Even here at this vast distance, beholding in his Word as in a glass the glory of the Lord, we are changed into the same image; the work of transformation and sanctification goes forward, though with much remaining imperfection. But there we shall be like him, for we shall see him as he is. To be with Jesus and to behold his glory is to be every moment drinking in with every sense the knowledge of him whom to know is eternal life. It is to be brought with no interposing hindrance into the most intimate communion and fellowship with him who is the overflowing fountain of all good, and by whom we shall be filled to the utmost of our ever-enlarging capacities with the fullness of God.

But we have not yet reached the limit of the Saviour's petition in the text. Though we have long since passed the boundary of all that the human mind can comprehend, or imagination can conceive, there is another particular yet to be added. We know not what we say when we utter it. We only feel that above these enrapturing heights of glory, of which we have been endeavoring to catch a faint and feeble glimpse, there rises yet another, higher and more glorious still.

When Jesus prays that his people may behold his glory, he means something more than that they should witness a spectacle, even with the added thought that this spectacle should produce a beneficial and transforming effect upon them. He means not to have them stand like Moses on the top of Pisgah to view afar the enchanting prospect of the Canaan he should never enter. To "see death" is in Scripture phrase not merely to witness it but to experience it; to "see corruption" is to become a prey to corruption; to "see sorrow" is to be sorrowful; to "see good days" is to have a glad and joyful time; to "see the kingdom of God" is to partake of its benefits; and to "behold Christ's glory" is to be a sharer of that glory. "The glory which thou hast given me," says Jesus, "I have given them." "To him that overcometh will I grant to sit with me in my throne, even as I also overcame, and am set down with my Father in his throne." The glory which beatified saints, behold, is their own. It is the glory of their Redeemer and their Saviour, achieved by him for them, bestowed by him upon them. They are one with him, and all that he has is theirs.

But we cannot scan, we cannot even trace the outline of these pinnacles of glory. The imagination reels and thought is bewildered, and the summits are hidden in the brightness of the throne itself. We cannot follow the luminous upward track of the ascending saint. He vanishes from our sight in the blaze of ever-accumulating glory. We only know that the petition is fulfilled, "Father, I will that they also, whom thou hast given me, be with me where I am, that they may behold my glory."

Brethren, pardon one additional word. This is the end which Jesus solicits for all his followers; this is the result which he has contemplated from the beginning; this is the design of all his work for them; this is the design of all his work in them; this is the burden of his intercessions on their behalf. Is this what we are living for, and striving after, and reaching unto—the center of our hopes, the object of our desires, the mark toward which our struggles are directed? Is our heart fixed not on an earthly but a heavenly aim, and does this enter into our daily and constant thoughts and plans, so that heaven seems to us not a violent rupture of all that precedes, a sudden stop to our pursuits, an abandonment of cherished plans, a reversal of all that we were engaged in, but rather its legitimate, expected, longed-for consequence, the last step forward in the direction that we have been urging our way, and which puts the proper finish to our whole lives. Is our treasure in heaven, or is it on the earth? The answer to this question will reveal to which world we belong, and in which world we shall take our portion.

THE PROMISE OF THE SPIRIT.

BY THE LATE PROF. CASPAR WISTAR HODGE, D.D., LL.D.

"*I have yet many things to say unto you, but ye cannot bear them now. Howbeit when he, the Spirit of truth, is come, he will guide you into all truth: for he shall not speak of himself; but whatsoever he shall hear, that shall he speak: and he will shew you things to come. He shall glorify me: for he shall receive of mine, and shall shew it unto you. All things that the Father hath are mine: therefore said I, that he shall take of mine, and shall shew it unto you.*"—JOHN 16:12-15.

CHRIST is to be glorified by the Spirit. He humbled himself in his incarnation, in assuming the form of a servant, and in submitting himself to death. This work is now accomplished. The Father is glorified in his obedience, and his reward remains. He is to go away, to go to the Father, to be glorified with that glory which he had before the world was made. The Spirit dwelling in his humanity, fills him with the power and the glory of God, so that what in his humiliation was the veil of Godhead, becomes in his exaltation its adequate expression. He fills heaven with the splendor of the presence of the glory of God, and is the object of the adoration of saints and angels. But the Spirit glorifies Christ not only in his personal exaltation, but in his Church: "He shall glorify me: for he shall take of mine, and shall show it unto you." The glory of Christ is to be manifested in the completion of his work of redemption. He has received the Spirit that he may give the Spirit to his Church. This is his ascension gift, which carries into execution the work which he came to do, and thus manifests his glory. The Spirit is to convince of sin, to work faith in men, to unite to Christ, to communicate his life, to procure the victory over the world, and to bring his people to the enjoyment of his glory in eternity.

The fundamental fact with regard to this work of the Holy Spirit is that it is accomplished by means of the truth. Christ describes it as a process of teaching. "He shall take of mine, and shall show it unto you." "I have yet many things to say unto you, but ye cannot bear them now. Howbeit when he, the Spirit of truth, is come, he will lead you into all truth." The Spirit, indeed, as a divine agent, acts immediately on the soul, imparts the principle of new life, determines the will, and influences the affections; but in all the conscious activities of the soul the truth is the instrument by which he works, and the sphere of all the activities of the new life. Jesus promises the Spirit to enable believers to keep his commandments; as such he is the "Spirit of truth, whom the world cannot receive, because it beholdeth him not, neither knoweth him, but ye know him, for he dwelleth in you." The indwelling Spirit is a spirit of knowledge. He promises the Spirit to unite to himself in order to fruit-bearing. And again, he says of the branches, in order to their fruitfulness, "Ye are clean through the word which I have spoken unto you." He is to give life; "and this is life eternal, that they might know thee, the only true God, and Jesus Christ, whom thou hast sent." The promise to prayer is conditioned on the revelation of his name. The mystical theory of religion, therefore, which depreciates the truths of revelation, and which claims priority for a divine love and obedience, in immediate contemplation and personal communion with God, arrays itself against the plain teaching of Christ. Because Christ identifies the truth which the Spirit is to bring with the truth which he taught. It is of the same character, and addressed to the intelligence, claiming faith, and operating practically on the conscience. He had taught them of the Father, and the Spirit was to carry on his teaching to completion in the same way. And the criterion for truth in the teaching is not the inward light, making every man a law to himself, or the Church as mediator of truth, but it is that what the Spirit is to communicate is the things of Christ. "He shall take of the things that are mine, and show them to you:" thus identifying his whole revelation of truth in his person and teaching with that which the Spirit should afterward communicate. To love this truth is to love the Spirit; to look away from the Scriptures for the truth is to give ear to other spirits, to whose teaching there is attached no promise of the revelation of the glory of the Lord.

I. In this supreme promise of our Saviour we see the unity of the dispensations. The salvation promised is wrought by Christ; and the Spirit secures it to every believer. Regeneration, sanctification, glorification, are his work, and this work is radiant with light and love, because it consists in bringing Christ to us, in binding us to him, and in making all our service to be replete with his presence and to tend to his glory.

II. In this promise we read clearly the basis of our faith in revelation, and in the inspiration of the writings of the New Testament. An acute commentator has remarked that at John 14: 25, 26 we

THE PROMISE OF THE SPIRIT. 33

have the warrant for the inspiration of the Gospels: "These things have I spoken unto you, being yet present with you. But the Comforter, which is the Holy Ghost, whom the Father will send in my name, he shall teach you all things, and bring all things to your remembrance, whatsoever I have said unto you." And here also is the warrant for the inspiration of the Epistles: "When he, the Spirit of truth, is come, he will guide you into all truth. . . . He shall take of mine, and shall show it unto you."

It is impossible to conceive how the authority of the Master could be conveyed to the teaching of the disciples more emphatically than is here done by Christ. He identifies his teaching and the teaching of the Spirit as parts of a whole: his teaching is carrying out my teaching; it is calling to remembrance what I have told you; it is completing what I have begun. And to make the unity emphatic, he explains why he had reserved so much of his own teaching, and committed the work of revelation to the Spirit. He, in his incarnation and life, comprised all saving truth. He was the revealer of God and the truth and the life. But while some things he had taught while yet with them, he had many things to say which must be postponed, because they could not bear them yet.

He had taught them of the spirituality of his kingdom, of its universal application, of the duties to God and man which it demanded, of the love of the Father in our salvation, of his own divine claims and the necessity of faith in him. He had taught them of the necessity of his dying in order to their coming glory; but they were so preoccupied with the notions of a temporal kingdom that they could not bear the conception of the cross. He had taught that his kingdom was for all men; but their Jewish pride could not brook the idea that salvation was by faith only, and on equal terms for all men; these truths they could not bear. There was the natural limitation of their receptivity to be estimated. The change from the old to the new order, the idea of the incarnation and of the kingdom to be established, were an intellectual revolution quite enough for one generation to receive and to realize. There were their Jewish prejudices to be considered, which colored all their conceptions, and perverted their apprehension of the truth which Christ taught. Besides this, the full conception of the relation of Christ's death to the doctrine of the Atonement could not be positively formulated until after his death had occurred; nor the adequate apprehension of his divine claims and mediatorial government attained until after the resurrection and the ascension had afforded the material facts upon which the doctrine was based. And still more, the outpouring of the Spirit at Pentecost was essential to illumine their minds and convey the promised inward strength, by which they could understand these stupendous truths. What is old to us was new to them; what is full of spiritual attraction to us required for them the renunciation of the most cherished hopes; what is to us most manifestly divine seemed to them to contradict the express teaching of their Scriptures. So Christ, as a wise teacher, imparted the germ of truth as they were able to bear it, and when he promised the Spirit to carry forward this teaching he made it impossible to conceive of it as differing in kind, or in any essential, except mode of revelation. He was to take of the things which were Christ's, and show them to the disciples.

That this promise to the disciples is specific, and constitutes them the inspired teachers of the Church after them, is proved first of all, (1) by the circumstances of Christ's address to them. They are in the upper chamber, at the last supper, separated from the body of believers, plunged in grief at the approaching separation. He tells them that his departure means his exaltation, and that his exaltation means his giving them the Spirit, who should teach them all things. He distinguishes them from others when he prays for them, and not for them only, but for all who should after believe "through their word."

(2) It is proved next by the whole history of their selection and separation from the body of disciples, to be witnesses for him, both of his resurrection and of his teaching. "The Comforter shall testify of me, and ye also shall bear witness, because ye have been with me from the beginning." "As the Father hath sent me into the world, so have I sent you into the world." "Whoso heareth you heareth me, and whosoever receiveth me receiveth him that sent me." "If they have not kept my saying, how shall they keep your word?" It is one of the central facts of the life of Christ that the work of founding and instructing the future Church was prepared for by the appointment of the body of Apostles, and the charism of the Spirit is but the necessary qualification for the work.

(3) It is seen further in the great commission specially given to the eleven, to go into all the world, "and teach all nations, baptizing them in the name of the Father, and of the Son, and of the Holy Ghost."

(4) It is seen still further in the scope of the

promise given to them. This is not simply to enlighten them, so that they would spiritually apprehend essential truth, so that their faith should not rest on human evidence but on the power of God. It is more than that the Spirit should so unfold the truth that they should be able to apprehend the love of God, and be sanctified and prepared for heaven. It is that they should complete his work. That primary revelation of truth, which was to be authoritative for the Church and demand the faith of all, and which he had only partially made, they were to make complete. The Spirit should take of the things which were his. And the measure and scope of this truth is stated: "All things that the Father hath are mine; therefore I said that he shall take of mine and shall show it unto you." Evidently whatever of divine truth is communicable, in its whole comprehensive scope and sublime elevation, is here conveyed. No human intellect can embrace the measure of this bestowment. No Christian Church can claim to have exhausted it. There are illimitable heights and depths here, which belong alone to the Divine Being, and can characterize a vehicle of truth only such as the Spirit of God himself can constitute. Which will you have, the Bible to open to you the eternal depths of the Divine Being, or the mystic's consciousness when he reduces to expression the summary of his feelings?

(5) But if on the one hand we find Christ giving authority to the disciples, and on the other the disciples after Pentecost assuming authority on the ground of Christ's appointment, the conclusion is irresistible that we must accept from them their own statement as to the nature and extent of their inspiration. It is therefore a perfectly logical position, as it is the only Scriptural position, that our doctrine of the inspiration of the writings is to be derived from the writings themselves. If Christ has referred us to the Apostles as teachers of the truths which he would have us know, certainly this primary truth of the authority of the Scriptures themselves can be no exception. All questions as to the extent of this inspiration, as to its exclusive authority, as to whether it extends to words as well as doctrines, as to whether it is infallible or inerrant or not, are simply questions to be referred to the Word itself. Whenever it claims authority we are bound to accord it absolute trust.

The question of inerrancy, which upon these principles must be reduced to the very narrowest limits, can be a question to be determined by observation only when it can be shown that it is covered by no claim of authority; for where an apostle makes that claim we must hear him as we would hear Christ. And that for the whole substance of the teaching, in the separate writings of the New Testament as well as in the New Testament as a whole, they do claim authority as the guides of faith, as the rule of life, can be denied only by very reckless assertion. We read it in the stress laid on the fact of their appointment by Christ; in the constant urgency with which Paul claims his equality on this point with the original apostles; in the express assertion, "I, Paul, an apostle, not of men, neither by man, but by Jesus Christ, and God the Father, who raised him from the dead." We read it in the constant demand for faith in their message and obedience to their injunctions. It is implied in their indignant rejection of all humanly devised error which would contradict or modify the Gospel as they had taught it: "If any man preach any other gospel unto you than that ye have received, let him be accursed. But I certify you, brethren, that the gospel which was preached of me is not after man, for I neither received it of man, neither was I taught it, but by the revelation of Jesus Christ." We see it in the whole conception of the Gospel as a body of revealed truth committed to them, and by them to the Church, which the

Church is bound to guard as its peculiar trust, and for the sake of which, specifically, the organization of the Church, with its specified offices, was instituted according to the Pastoral Epistles. We read it most clearly in Paul's argument in 1 Corinthians, where he contrasts the validity and effect of revealed truth with the speculations of philosophy: "Now we have received, not the spirit of the world, but the Spirit which is of God; that we might know the things that are freely given to us of God. Which things also we speak, not in the words which man's wisdom teacheth, but which the Holy Ghost teacheth; combining spiritual things with spiritual;" i.e., spiritual truths with spiritual words. We see it in the miraculous attestations to which apostles appealed to support their claim of supernatural authority. And we see it in the unity of the Scriptures; in the accord of apostolic teaching with the teaching of Christ; in the historic development of the revelation, in accord with the existing wants of the churches; in the whole tone of divinity, as with tenderness and fidelity the divine oracles open to us the deep things of God. It is one kind of religion to make the divine Word the test of our characters, and to be enabled by the Spirit to recognize its divine quality. It is a very different kind of religion to bring the Bible to the test of our religious feelings, and to decide whether or not it is of God by its accord with the responses of those feelings.

III. The New Testament doctrine of the Canon bases itself on the authority of Christ in this promise. Those books which by clear historical proof can be shown to have belonged to the collection given by the apostles to the churches, or in their separate issue to have been given by them as the revelation of truth, come to us with the authority of the apostles, and their authority conveys to us the sanction of the Lord. As was the Old Testament to him, so he gives us the New Testament for our guidance. We are constantly told that this is antiquated; that it is mere traditionalism; that the new Apologetic is based upon our recognition of Christ in the Word; and that the Bible is truth to us because "it finds us." Thank God if it finds us! So does Tennyson find us, and so do Shakespeare and Seneca and Sophocles. If we are to judge by the opposition to some of the distinctive doctrines of the Bible, it is only part of it that "finds us." It finds us when it tells us that we are weak and need help; but when it tells us we are guilty and need forgiveness, we are not so sure of it. It finds us when it offers a better life and a better hope; but when it declares the righteous judgment of God on all sin, the response becomes very weak. It finds us when we read of the universal Fatherhood of God, of the unfathomable love, of the helpful sympathy of Christ; but when it tells of the resplendent justice on which the creature cannot look and live, or of the atoning sacrifice, or of the sovereignty of grace, there is no inward response. This new conception of God, to which the milder and more loving theology of this end of the century has come, is not the God of the Bible. The New Testament only has given us Jesus Christ. Surely we cannot, on the claim of the authority of Christ, reject the authority of the New Testament!

IV. The promise of the Spirit is the promise of spiritual illumination to all believers. It is confessedly difficult in the interpretation of this discourse of our Saviour to distinguish accurately what applies to apostles only, and what to the Church at large; what conveys the promise of inspiration, and what of spiritual illumination to all believers. And yet the distinction is essential; for if it be disregarded, if the promises of revelation and inspiration be applied to all believers, the authority of the apostles and their writings is reduced to the common level of the religious thought of men of peculiar genius and peculiar advantages; or, on the other hand, the inward light common to all is elevated to equal or superior authority to the Word of God. It is, however, in analogy with the general teaching of Christ that his doctrine of the work of the Spirit should be given in the germ, and not unfolded; in its broad outlines, and not specialized. And as we have found clear evidence that some of these words can be realized in their full sense only in the inspiration of the apostles, so we find no less clear proof that the supreme gift of the Spirit is not confined to them.

And this proof consists, first, in the fact that he assigns to the work of the Spirit now promised the imparting of the Christian life, in all its graces which are the common heritage of all believers. The Spirit, who is to lead us into truth, is thereby to unite us to Christ; to constitute the life of Christ in his Church; to bring to us the love of the Father; to enable us to believe in Christ; to work in us obedience to his will; to secure the hearing of prayer; to cause us to bring forth fruit unto God; to gain the victory over the world; and, finally, to bring us to the beatific vision of God in the better life. Obviously, the promise is not exclusively to the apostles.

The second proof is the close relation between

the spiritual illumination, which is common to all, and the superadded revelation and inspiration, which is promised to the apostles. They need this spiritual knowledge and personal apprehension of the truth before they can convey it to others. It is no mechanical but a living force that lifts them to heights of view of divine things whence they discern the glories of Christ and convey them to us. In his measure—not of authority to others, not as the teacher of the whole Church, but for his own spiritual satisfaction—the humblest Christian has in kind the same knowledge of the divine power and light and grace which is in the Word of Christ as had Paul or John.

And thirdly, as before, the promise of authority to the apostles points us to their own teaching for the fuller unfolding of the distinction between that grace of the knowledge of the Spirit, which is common and necessary for all, and those peculiar gifts which make their writings authoritative.

These truths, which only the Spirit can communicate, can only be apprehended by the Spirit. Precisely their divine quality, which separates them from all other deliverances of truth, is only apprehended by a divine influence in the soul. The life-giving power, which conveys faith and love and hope, which goes from the particular truth to the relations and sees the harmonies and beauties of the whole, which sees in the Word in all its parts the revelation of the Father and the glory of the Son, is by spiritual discernment. This blessed gift, comprehending all gifts, is thus the unity of the Christian life, bringing Christ to dwell in us; and through the instrumentality of the Word, by the authority of the Scriptures, it works out our complete salvation, for "He takes of the things that are Christ's, and shows them unto us."

Your future ministry is cast in times of great theological unrest. Foundations are broken up; truths long accepted are brought anew into question; the very principles upon which the certitude of belief is to rest are under debate. There is no use in these days for men of a light and easy temper, who make up their judgment hastily on the most vital questions, or who like to be in the advance of all changes, and easily renounce the most sacred of heritages. Men should be sober and thoughtful; they should be students of history; they should be prayerful students of the Bible. Change is not necessarily advance. The majestic testimony of the Church in all time is that its advances in spiritual life have always been toward and not away from the Bible, and in proportion to the reverence for, and power of realizing in practical life, the revealed Word. The watchword of the modern school is, on every hand, "Back to Christ!" Surely we say "Amen!" From every departure of thought or life, let us go back to Christ. But it is one thing to realize afresh the life and teaching of Christ in the historic spirit, in relation to what is to come, as the germinal planting of a future harvest of life and doctrine; it is a very different thing to go back to Christ by the rejection of all subsequent revelation, which is based on his authority and is the living development of his teaching. They tell us that it is not the "Christ of the creeds" to whom we should go. "The Church has lost the Spirit of Christ," it is said, "because she has attended to the doctrines about him, confining her conception in scholastic forms, disputing about consubstantiality, and person, and nature, and satisfaction to justice, and thereby losing the living pulse of sympathy and love and practical life in his teaching." So far as the Church has sacrificed life to mere theological science, it is to be repented of and amended. But when the process of generalization and definition and coördination of Scripture facts is sneered at, the charge is simple puerility; and when the assertion is that logical definition has interfered with reverential love and obedience, it is reckless slander of the Spirit-led history of the Church of Christ.

We are pointed back of the Christ of the Church theology to the Christ of the New Testament. But we cannot stop there. Because the Christ of Paul is not the living and personal Christ, but a person of theological debate. The questions of preëxistence, of revelation, of humiliation, of exaltation—especially the legal aspect of his work, satisfying justice and working righteousness—have begun this process of "disastrous disfigurement" of the sacred things, which the Church has carried onward. We must not rest in apostolic conceptions, but go back to the fountain-head, the historic Christ of the Gospels. But even here the Christ of John has already begun to be overlaid with foreign speculative elements. Tender, sublime, spiritual, offering mystical union and exalting love indeed, but at the same time asserting with unfaltering authority his equality with God, asserting that life depends on faith in him, magnifying the divine sovereignty and efficacious grace. Here are speculative elements which may interfere with the simplicity and truth of the figure, and we therefore come back to the Christ of the Synoptic Gospels. But there we are cautioned that these Gospels were written late in the life of the Church, and we must carefully distinguish between what Christ really did and taught, and what is ascribed to him by the growing misconception of the Church theology. And when, at last, we have reached this teaching, rich, profound, divine, containing in germinal form the whole of the truth afterward communicated by the Spirit, we are still further taught that we must discriminate carefully in the teaching of Christ himself between what belongs merely to the prejudices of his day and generation, and the message that he is commissioned of God to impart. He comes not with infallible revelation, teaching the things of God out of his conscious omniscience, we are told; but one tells us that his Messianic consciousness grows out of his consciousness of ethical oneness with God; and another that it is an inference from his universal love for men and his desire for their salvation. In the one sphere he is not only limited in knowledge, but may be entirely mistaken. In the other sphere he brings to us the truth which is our life. And we are to distinguish, by the light within, what is really of Christ and what is not.

We, on our part, accept this motto, "Back to Christ." And as his parting word, we hear him tell the disciples that he would send the Spirit, who should lead them into all truth. We, on this authority, accept the teaching of Paul and John concerning him. And so far as the Church has by this promised guidance unfolded the truth of revelation, we accept her interpretation of the Scriptures. Here is the New Testament criterion of truth. Here is Christ's most sacred parting legacy. Here is our choice of method. Which do you choose, *Christ* or *Barabbas?* Away from Christ, as imparted by the Spirit, we may not have the life he promises. For his promise to the Church to be with it alway to the end of the world is *by* that Holy Spirit.

VALIANT FOR THE TRUTH.

BY THE LATE PROF. CHARLES A. AIKEN, PH.D., D.D.

> "*And they bend their tongues like their bow for lies: but they are not valiant for the truth upon the earth; for they proceed from evil to evil, and they know not me, saith the Lord.*"—
> JEREMIAH 9:3.

THE reading of the Revised Version gives us a slight change in the form of the rendering, without altering essentially the conception: "And they are grown strong in the land, but not for truth; for they proceed from evil to evil, and they know not me, saith the Lord."

If the fact be so, and the prophet's arraignment of his people be true, his bitter grief is abundantly justified. The omen is of evil, and evil only. Let it be from ignorance, mistake, moral imbecility, cowardice, or a more positive and flagrant disloyalty, when men are strong, but not for the truth, valiant, but not for the truth, the sign is of present evil and greater evil to come. Therefore the prophet would seek in the wilderness a lodging-place of wayfaring men, where, his head waters and his eyes a very fountain of tears, he might weep for the slain of the daughters of his people.

You have not forgotten how fine a picture Bunyan sketches in his "Pilgrim's Progress" of one who is "valiant for truth." It is just as Christiana and her children are entering upon the eighth and last step of their pilgrimage that Greatheart and his company overtake this hero. Refusing to join the three who had beset him, Wildhead, Inconsiderate and Pragmatic, refusing also to go back at their bidding, he had fought them and put them to flight, caring nothing for numbers, because "little or more are nothing to him that has the truth on his side"; praying to his king, "who I knew could hear me and afford invisible help, and that was sufficient for me"; using confidently and to good purpose "the right Jerusalem blade in his hand, with which one may venture upon an angel"; at the same time, with the practical earnestness and energy that come of faith, clinging to his sword-hilt with a grip so firm that the blood ran through his fingers; and when he was asked to give account of his former life, summing up all by saying, "I believed, and therefore came out and got into the way, fought all that set themselves against me, and by believing am come to this place." Plainly, whatever his valor might be he knew and proclaimed that its spring was in his faith. This is the type of character which our text by contrast brings before us. Over such a robust and valorous faith there were no need to weep one's eyes away in the wilderness.

It may be worth our while to study this type of character in four aspects: (1) In its relation to the nature, rights, and claims of truth; (2) in its relation to the highest capacities, dignities, and responsibilities of manhood; (3) in its relation to the just call and sore peril of souls about us that may be saved, perhaps saved by one valiant for the truth while no other strength or valor would help them; and (4) in its relation to our professed loyalty to Jesus Christ.

Let it be borne in mind all along the line of our thought that we cannot come even into quiet possession of the truth without overcoming the opposition of forces, within and without, which would keep us from it; that we cannot, except by a high and sustained valor, bring our own lines into true and full conformity to the truth where so much is to be accomplished in molding character and life into this likeness, and where antagonism is so stubborn; that after we have gained the truth and begun to put on the image of the truth, we are not to be left in peace in the enjoyment of our possession and its benefits, but must maintain every acquisition at the point of the sword; that we are bound to support actively and aggressively truth's claim to a universal dominion; that even in the sorest exigencies of our own experience we are never for a moment absolved from the obligation to remember and care for others' needs and perils; and that the glorious Captain of our salvation deserves and demands the service of good soldiers, each striving "that he may please him who enrolled him as a soldier." And let us further keep in mind that valor is nourished and sustained by truth, for which there is no possible equivalent or substitute.

"Valiant for truth." What, then, is truth, that for it one can be, should be, valiant? Truth is real. Truth is accessible and may be known. Truth is precious. Truth imposes in every direction obligations that cannot be met except by the most genuine and resolute valor.

If Horne Tooke was right in his etymology, truth would seem to be one of the most uncertain, unreliable of things, or the instinct to have been in this case strangely at fault by which names are given to things. He tells us that truth is primarily *what one troweth*. To trow is to think, believe, or suppose. What the world "troweth" is as variable, doubtful and unsubstantial as diversities of power, opportunity, diligence, fidelity, sanity can make it. The best philologists of our own generation, however, refer the word to a root meaning, "to believe," and draw upon the whole group of related languages and dialects to show that truth is "firm, strong, solid, reliable, anything that will hold." It should seem, then, that we ought not to believe anything but what is firm, established, and that truth is what we rightly believe. We are not playing with words. To the Hebrew thought expressing itself in word-building, truth is something that has stability, that is fixed and sure. To the Greek it is the unconcealed reality of that which had been veiled. If this is truth, we have in it something to strive after, something to stand on, something to offer to and urge upon others that is better than a waking fancy or a dream of the night. We accept this judgment of the great mind of the race—Hebrew, Greek, Germanic—and hold that truth is the real, the established, the abiding. For this our highest powers can be summoned into action, while nothing but a poor counterfeit of our best activity can be called forth in behalf of that which is known or seriously suspected to be unreal. The sophist may be adroit, dexterous in disposition and argument, and selfishly eager for victories. The pettifogging advocate in any profession may gain brief successes by natural powers and discipline, aided by sheer audacity. This is a result and proof of the world's disorder. Man is for truth and truth for man—both real.

And truth is accessible and may be known. No agnostic can be a Valiant for Truth. Quixotic endeavors after the unattainable may supply entertaining reading for idle hours, or possibly suggest curious studies in psychology. Our curiosity, busy and scheming, impertinent and sometimes impious, may direct its adventures toward lofty and distant realms that are not for us. Our real and serious and right concern is rather with the truth that is near, inviting and demanding knowledge, threatening our indifference or neglect with serious loss or heavy penalty. The realms are broad enough the natural reason may traverse, incited by higher motives, cheered by brighter prospects, than ever girded and sent out King Arthur's knights, or any other heroes of the days of chivalry. But natural reason is not the only discoverer of truth, nor is nature its only depository. Fossils buried for uncounted ages in the rocks are not its only prophets. No biological analysis can reach all its elements: no scientific imagination can construct its entire fabric. The statistician cannot tabulate all its facts. Philosophers, in the endless involutions and evolutions of their speculations, miss much of it. He who gave us reason and nature, whose they are, and whom they should ever serve, has come in pity to the relief of our impotence and bewilderment by the disclosures that his Spirit makes. When we ask for bread he does not answer us with stones and reptiles only, and bid us get our sustenance from them. He comes down to us from above, not always and only up to us from below. To abase the swelling pride that loves to contemplate itself as standing at the top of the long development of being, he tells us of sin and helplessness and ruin, and then of love and grace and salvation. In the Gospel "the grace of God that bringeth salvation hath appeared unto all men."

Here is truth that is real. Here is truth that may be known. Of all precious truth, truth on which souls can be nourished, truth to which lives can be safely conformed, here is that which is most precious—truth that enters most deeply and permanently into character and takes hold of destiny. Of all truth worthy and suited to stimulate man's highest powers to the most sustained and most intense efficiency, here is that which is worthiest and most suited. Of all truth that is of such kind and in such relations to us that it is not only worth our while, but in every way incumbent upon us to put forth our highest valor to gain it and to hold it, here is the most essential.

We are bidden, "Buy the truth and sell it not." And this is not a mere appeal to our self-interest. It is not left to the decision of our taste whether truth shall attract and please us or not. It is not submitted to our mere option in any way. The world's wise men might mean no more than this by the proverb. But what the wisdom of inspiration commends, the divine authority commands; thus we gain the truth at whatever cost, and never part with it at any price. Truth, especially this sacred truth, encompasses us with obligations. For this acquisition we do not merely do well to pay the price of toil and struggle; we fail grossly and widely in duty if we withhold the price. And what we have so dearly bought at the price of our humbled pride, at the price of our falling out with the fashion of this world "which passeth away," what we win by the surrender of our self-sufficiency and imaginary independence, by our resolute self-mastery, our vigorous effort, and whatever besides the attainment may cost, we are to hold against all seductions and all assaults, "valiant for the truth."

Our second question was to be: What is the manly valor that can find any fair and proper field for its exercise—its fairest and most proper field in connection with truth? What is the relation of truth on the one side to valor, and on the other to manhood? Valor, a word that carries us back so easily to the days and the deeds of knightly prowess, adventure and achievement, starts with the primary idea of health and strength. It is not mere boldness, bravery, courage, but moves in a higher plane, and is instinct with a loftier inspiration. These may have their source chiefly in the physical and animal, that which we share with the bull-dog and the gorilla; while valor is a knightly grace, and makes account mainly of the ideal. Medieval chivalry was sometimes fantastic in its manifestations. Yet in those centuries which intervened between general barbarism and our modern civilization it did much to lift men out of their grossness. It was a fighting grace; yet it had much to do with the whole character. To be a valiant soldier was more than to be robust and fearless. Of course we recognize different types and degrees of valor, as well as different spheres and occasions for its exercise. We shall esteem that the truest valor in which there is the fullest consciousness and manifestation of manhood, with the clearest conception and the most persistent adherence to worthy ends of manly endeavor. There can then be nothing forced or unnatural in the phrase of our text, "valiant for the truth."

For what should a true man be valiant rather than for the acquisition, maintenance, and service of the truth—truth known as real, judged to be important, valued as precious? And what estimate must we put upon the manhood that can be "strong in the land, but not for truth"—energetic, daring, resolved, and persistent for lower and grosser interests, but not for the truth? The manhood that is most sound and healthy recognizes most promptly and broadly its relationship to truth, knows its affinity for truth, responds most heartily to the claim and challenge of the truth, enlists with the least of hesitation or reserve in the search for the service of the truth. "A man who will take the world easily will never take it grandly," we are told. An ambitious manhood sees in connection with the truth prizes most worthy of its ambition. A courageous manhood, if it might choose its sphere, would ask to show itself in behalf of so good a cause, where the difficulties and perils, and the success, mean so much. For this it will most patiently and thoroughly discipline itself, and toil most strenuously. It knows that it is vindicating and honoring itself by the same activities by which it is most exalting truth. It can most easily, gladly and completely forget itself and make least account of toils and pains and cost when maintaining the cause of truth or promoting some interest of our fellow-men in connection with the truth. And this choice and devotion find a quick and large reward, as truth ministers to the manliness that offers its best in its behalf, the richest rewards coming, of course, from the highest moral and spiritual truth. The truth that stands nearest to Christ has the best right to say, "Them that honor me I will honor."

But looking beyond ourselves, beyond results anticipated for ourselves, beyond obligations that bind us in our own behalf, by what call from without does truth most authoritatively and effectively summon valor to its aid? This was to be our third inquiry. "Victory in a tournament" of olden time, the historian Hallam tells us, "was little less glorious, and perhaps at the moment more exquisitely felt, than in the field, since no battle could assemble such witnesses of valor." This does not mean that the display of valor before the assembled beauty and rank of courts was valued above valor itself. The valor must exist to be displayed. And before we condemn the motive as wholly ignoble we should recall to mind the appeal with which the twelfth chapter of Hebrews opens: "Wherefore, seeing we also are compassed about with so great a cloud of witnesses." These displays of valor on the tented field were accounted an augury of triumphs to be won on fields where graver issues were at stake; where some imperiled life or treasure was to be rescued, some essential but questioned honor to be vindicated, some great wrong to be redressed, some grand right to be gained or defended. It was not mere and weak sentiment that strove to recover the Holy Land or some sacred shrine from the hands of the Paynim, or that followed the banner of one's liege lord or the standard of the cross to new conquests. It was worth much to all coming ages that high ideals should be brought down into the gross lives of men and made efficient there.

The first appeals which truth makes to us, the first obligations which it imposes on us, are in its own behalf and our own behalf. We are first to make this rich endowment our own. Here is a treasure that we gain by finding it and submitting ourselves to it. We do not command, but surrender. Our command is consequent upon and proportionate to our obedience, our success to our submission. And the valor that is called into requisition before this result is reached is real and of the finest quality. We have the truth only when it possesses us. All other mastery must be dislodged, all other dominion cast off. The effort by which we gain, and the grasp with which we hold the truth, or rather with which it holds us, mean the overcoming of many natural and moral difficulties and opportunities. Indolence is to be mastered, and all the bias of one's nature to evil and error. Stubborn habits are to be broken up, riotous and groveling tastes subdued. Many a breach is to be made and carried in the walls of prejudice and evil association, many an abstraction swept away, many a foe vanquished. A good soldier he will have proved himself who has surrendered and subjected himself fully to the truth. But we are not at liberty to look no further than to our own enrichment with the amplest treasures of wisdom and knowledge, and enlargement of our own natures, and invigoration of our own powers, the manifold satisfactions, enjoyments, and dignities that come to us with and by the truth.

Truth is imperial, not only in the quality of the authority which it asserts and the richness of the bounty which it dispenses, but also in the breadth of the dominion to which it lays claim. We have made our first obedience when we have yielded ourselves to the truth. We are to go on proclaiming truth's rights, and helping it to gain rule over others. We vindicate the rights of the truth while we secure blessings to our fellow-men through truth's ascendency over them. And this obligation and opportunity subject our manhood to some of the most searching tests by which we are ever tried. Are we capable of taking larger views of truth than those which connect it with some prospect of advantage to ourselves? Do we esteem it for what it is, and not only for what it brings us? And what is the measure of our discernment of the rights and needs of others—and what is our response? His is a poor starveling manhood that cannot be stirred to interest and effort and sacrifice in the assertion of others' rights and the promotion of their good. The knightly spirit prompted as much as this; shall the Christian spirit be content with less? There is a natural largeness of soul that can appreciate others' jeopardy, and stir itself to avert or relieve it. A low and common nature is dull of sense to all these calls from without. It puts narrow interpretations on those obligations which it cannot wholly disown. The manly and Christian spirit has large conceptions of right and duty.

And then truth, while imperial in its rights, is sometimes imperiled by denial and attack, and that at the hands of the very men whose allegiance it claims. Its rights are contested; its very credentials are challenged. It encounters not merely the negative resistance of ignorance and dullness, of low tastes and sensual and earthly preoccupations; it is met by a more positive impeachment. He who is valiant for truth will no more suffer it to fight its own battles than a true knight would have resorted to any such evasion in a cause to which he was committed. And the response which we make to the summons of assailed truth gives opportunity to display some of the finest qualities that belonged to the old knighthood—unswerving loyalty, courage, endurance, self-sacrifice.

Both New Testament and Old Testament emphasize this part of a good soldier's duty toward sacred truth. "Fight the good fight of faith," "knowing that I am set for the defense of the Gospel." "Wherefore, take unto you the whole armor of God, that ye may be able to withstand in the evil day." "Stand, therefore." Across an interval of many centuries more, perhaps from the time of Sennacherib's siege of Jerusalem, come those stirring words of the forty-eighth Psalm: "Walk about Zion, and go round about her: tell the towers thereof; mark ye well her bulwarks." She needs and has her towers and bulwarks, and there is for us a post of duty there at the defense of truth. If Paul the aggressive evangelist is an example for study and imitation, Paul the apologist is no less so. Our broader study of questioned truth brightens many an evidence, confirms many a conviction, kindles a new enthusiasm for the assertion and defense of truth's claim, and subjects to new tests our professions of devotion. It puts to the proof our aptness, while it calls forth our energy. But truth is never content to stand long on the defensive. The defense is soon turned into attack. Error may be content with compromise; truth is satisfied with nothing less than established dominion.

But there is another call for valor in behalf of Christian truth higher than that which comes from our fellow-men and their claims upon it. What Christ is on the one side to the truth and on the other side to us, and what the truth is to him, supply a new inspiration and strength, and add a new quality to Christian endeavor—a personal quality that was wanting before. He who is valiant for the truth because of what it is in its reality and reliableness shows his discernment. He who is valiant for the truth because of what it is to manhood shows a wise self-appreciation. He who is valiant for the truth because of the claim his fellow-men have upon it, and upon him if he has it in his possession, shows that he knows his place, his obligation, his opportunity as a man among men. He who is valiant for the truth for Christ's sake shows that he knows and honors his Lord, and would make him indeed Lord of all.

Consider what Christ is to the substance of the truth; what he is to the authority and efficiency of the truth; and what the truth is to him in the assertion and manifestation of his Lordship.

The truth is not only Christ's as its great Revealer; the truth is Christ as its great revelation. "I am the way, and the truth, and the life." If we invert each of these phrases, we are not unsound in logic or false to fact. To him who asks, What is the way? we answer, *The way* is Christ. To him who would know, What is the life? we make reply, *The life* is Christ. And we proclaim, as that which is of the highest concern to man to know, *the truth* is Christ. He is the great embodiment of truth—truth incarnate. What he was, over and above all that he said, teaches us what we should seek in vain to learn elsewhere. He was the chief revelation of the nature, the power, the love, the saving grace of God. What is God?

What is holiness? What is redemption for sinners? He did not simply speak as never man spake on these high themes. We look to, we lay hold upon, himself, and find that he is made of God unto us wisdom and righteousness and sanctification and redemption. This is not bold metaphor merely; it is assured fact. "He that hath seen me hath seen the Father." We are "complete in him." "In whom" (not merely by receiving and following information that he supplies) "we have our redemption through his blood, and forgiveness of our trespasses, according to the riches of his grace." He did indeed bear a witness above all other witness to the truth. "To this end was I born, and for this cause came I into the world, that I should bear witness to the truth." But his witness was more in what he was and what he did than in all that he said. "Grace and truth came" (not "were given" as the law "was given" by Moses) by Christ. How this adds to the authority and to the efficiency of the truth! And see what use he makes of the truth. By it he tests and measures men: his disciples, "He that is of the truth heareth my voice," the voice of the Teacher, the voice of the Truth; his enemies, "Because I tell you the truth, ye believe me not." They reject in one act the truth and him, and show what they are. When he shall enter on his high and awful function as judge, peopling two worlds as he says, "Come, ye blessed! Depart, ye cursed!" it is according to the treatment of the truth that he makes his award. "Unto them that are factious and obey not the truth, but obey unrighteousness, shall be wrath and indignation, tribulation and anguish."

Meanwhile it is largely by the instrumentality of the truth that those who are his are made holy— "Seeing you have purified your souls in your obedience to the truth." His Church, "the Church of the living God," is declared to be "the pillar and ground of the truth." This it can never be by a mere passive support and upholding of a truth imposed. The Church (ἐκκλησία) is a body "called out" by God's heralds, his Spirit, his Son, to abide, to stand, to be established. But however stable, the living Church of the living God, intrusted with the upholding of his living truth, must have in exercise all that is active, forceful, courageous, and aggressive in the Christian life.

And therefore, because of the fullness and significance of the several representations of what Christ is to the truth, and the truth to Christ, it is all the more manifest that they who are loyal to Christ will be for this reason and in this measure valiant for the truth. We do no violence to the words of the sixtieth Psalm when we give them this specific application: "Thou [O Christ] hast given a banner to them that fear thee, that it may be displayed because of the truth." The banner is a symbol of union and allegiance, a rallying-point for the mustering or moving host, a continual source of inspiration. Moses, after the battle with Amalek, built an altar, and called the name of it Jehovah-nissi ("The Lord," i.e., Jehovah, "is my banner"). Those whose banner is not only the Lord's, but the Lord himself, cannot need any higher summons or motive to be valiant for the truth. This will be to the grateful, loving, loyal Christian the motive of motives—that Christ, his Lord, is what he is to the truth, and that the truth is what it is to Christ.

In our day, however, many influences are at work to neutralize the effect of all these considerations and appeals. There are subtle and plausible philosophies in vogue, and not among the learned only, that would make it absurd and preposterous to be very confident, or much in earnest in behalf of the truth. Pilate's question is popular: What is truth? and it is pressed upon us persistently from many sides with a sinister emphasis. For there are those who doubt, and there are those who teach men to doubt, whether there are any reliable criteria of truth—whether there is for us any certain truth. And there are others whose materialistic faith reduces to a paltry minimum the worth of truth. Then there is the theoretical secularism and the practical secularism, that would have us waive these doubtful and fruitless questionings in view of the reality, the nearness, the urgency of those material necessities and interests that demand, for ourselves and for others, all our thoughts and all our efficiency. It is not the hoarse clamor of the commune only which insists that the ideal and the spiritual must wait until more practical problems are solved. The infatuation of pleasure, the idolatry of gain, stifle in many more even the power of appreciating enthusiasm and earnestness in behalf of truth.

In another quarter another class of untoward influences is at work, and the issue of the working is not yet in sight. A belief is professed in higher things, in the reality and importance of truth, in respect to which one may possibly have deep and strong convictions, *provided* he does not in any way by word or deed give too vehement or repeated expression to it. The air is full of the praises of catholicity and toleration. Some hold it presumptuous, others grossly discourteous, others schismatic, that confidence should be expressed and earnestness manifested in anything that goes beyond the commonplaces of truth. Platitudes are admissible to any extent. Clear-cut faiths firmly held, vigorously defended, energetically urged upon others, are unfashionable. We know, however, of a Broad Churchism, that is tolerant not merely of diversities but of contradictions, that would remand zeal of a type exhibited by prophets and apostles to the centuries that are well left behind. We have heard pleadings for a thing so good in itself, and in measure good for so many practical reasons, as Christian union, which we find ourselves compelled to watch with double scrutiny since they would reduce to such a minimum the truth that we may be allowed to profess and proclaim, and for which we are permitted to be valiant, and since from that minimum so much is excluded that has been in the past so inspiring to Christian hope, so sustaining to Christian strength and heroism. This is an evil day for polemics and scholastics, and dogmatists and denominationalists. The only man who may be valiant without falling into disrepute is the irenic; he may be as dogmatic and combative as you please. We involuntarily call to mind the unpopularity of Elijah, the troubler of Israel, with Ahab. In the view of some there are no other troublers of Israel like the persistent, aggressive believers in truth.

And on still another side constant pressure is put upon us to suppress part of our witness to the truth. The world is a great believer in the doctrine of the invisible Church—the Church that does not show the power of the truth and its own unswerving loyalty to the truth by the conformity of its life to the truth. We may be allowed to believe what we are constrained to believe—or what we please—if only we do not let the truth too much change our conduct. Our creed may be the longest and the hardest and the most obnoxious, if we will conduct our business according to the maxims and methods of the world —entertain ourselves with its amusements, follow its capricious and imperious fashions. If there is no very noticeable difference in life between the Church and the world, the world will not so much trouble itself about our belief, except now and then slyly to propose the pertinent question, how we reconcile our conduct to our creed. Here, again, is a field in which Christian valor has an opportunity to show itself, in vindicating the right of truth, and illustrating the power of truth to rule the life. In some social circles this is the severest test to which Christian valor is subjected.

In view of all this we ask, Has "Valiant for

Truth," then, had his day? May we say for him no more than "Peace to his ashes"?

In our national and social affairs a wholesome, timely, and needed reaction has begun to set in against the false catholicity that was undermining the public welfare. Patriotism and statesmanship have begun to deal at various points with the question whether we have not swung open somewhat too widely the doors of our national hospitality. Our loud invitation—"Ho, every one!"—has gone beyond the limits of public safety. We are watching somewhat more closely the immigrants across the two great oceans. We begin to question whether we are equal to the entertainment, government and assimilation of such a mixed multitude, who fall a-lusting so soon and so grossly after liberties and indulgences that are so strange, intolerable and abhorrent to us. We object to the emptying upon our shores of the poorhouses and prisons and slums and lazarettos of the Old World; we send back the imported refuse, and hold the importers responsible. Economists, and not demagogues of labor only, are writing on our statute-books restrictions upon the unlimited importation of foreign labor. Propositions are pending, or are awaiting introduction in our national Senate, against the free admission of anarchists and the deluded converts of Mormon emissaries. We have been stirred to a new vigilance in behalf of our Christian and Puritan Sabbath, our social purity, our temperate temperance. Our religious press, our home missionary societies, our Evangelical Alliance, are arousing us to consider what a vast work we have already accumulated upon our hands.

Let the good work go on. Let it make us watchful in the sphere of our religious life. The sons of Covenanters and Pilgrims and Huguenots—and these were they that laid the foundations both of Church and State among us—should not too readily and cheaply sell their birthright, or sleep while it is stolen from them. What would they have been, what should we have been, but for this love of truth and this valor for the truth? We must learn how to enlarge our love without expense to our faith; how to find and keep the unity of the Spirit in the bond of peace without the surrender of truth. And in proportion as needs are multiplied and intensified we must be only the more loyal to the truth and its Lord, and valiant for it and for him.

SALVATION AS A WORK.

By Prof. William M. Paxton, D.D., LL.D.

"Being confident of this very thing, that he which hath begun a good work in you will perform it until the day of Jesus Christ."—Philippians 1:6.

WORK is the subject of this text. The world is full of busy work; the din of toil and the hum of industry is ever in our ears. But there is another work. Simultaneous with this work of the world, mingling with it, but rising above it in grandeur and importance, is another work—a divine work—a work for the salvation of souls. It is a work that has a strange secret of power. It is unseen and mysterious. It interpenetrates the world's work and often overreaches it. It draws men more effectually than the attractions of the world's enjoyments. It often separates them from worldly gains by the motive of more enduring riches. This work is going on busily amidst the world's active industries. Its agencies are organized; wherever men gather in the market-place, there is one to say, "Go ye into the vineyard." A divine message is meeting men in every avenue of life. The merchant hears it on 'Change, and stops to repeat the mysterious sound, "Lay up for yourself treasures in heaven." The farmer stops his plow in the furrow as he listens to the strange words, "Break ye up the fallow ground, and sow to yourselves in righteousness." The workman amidst the din and clank of machinery hears a still small voice, more penetrating than the din of toil, "Turn ye, turn ye, why will ye die?" The swift trains freighted with a nation's merchandise bear with them the agencies of the Gospel. The ships that carry the world's commerce carry also the missionary and the Bible to extend this work to the ends of the earth.

This work is not only, like the world's work, external, but also invisible, secret, and mysterious. It is a work in the souls of men, quickening, renewing, transforming. It generates a new life, forms a new character, and lifts man into alliance with God. Oh, there is nothing more sublime than to think that amidst all the noise and turmoil of the outward world this busy and mysterious work is silently going on in the souls of men, assimilating them to the divine image, and preparing upon this earth the great family of God and the kingdom of heaven.

SALVATION AS A WORK.

This is the work that is presented to us in the text. *Salvation as a work* is here described in a minute and beautiful detail.

I. *It is a good work.* "He who hath begun a *good work* in you will perform it until the day of Jesus Christ."

It is good in its experience. Nothing is so delightful as salvation, nothing else brings such present enjoyment, or so meets the wants and desires of our troubled and agitated spirits. In every other work we wander in disquietude through the circuit of humanity, but this brings us at once to the Creator, and, having found the center of rest and satisfaction, we wander no more.

One distinguished for knowledge and wisdom records his experience of salvation thus: "So long as I strove after earthly good and earthly wisdom there was in this striving nothing but restlessness and disquiet; but now in the hope of salvation all my cares and desires have become so tranquilized that there is continual peace." To this he adds: "I long thought that life ceased when religion began; but, behold! I have found that then first I lived when I began to love" (Tholuck). Such, indeed, is salvation with every one in whom the good work is truly experienced. They only then begin to live. The past, with all that they called pleasure and enjoyment, seems unworthy to be called life. The new life is so much higher and nobler, its pulses beat with such an intenser thrill, and its issues of love, joy and hope impart such a present, conscious bliss, that they seem as if waking up for the first time to real existence. The sun shines brighter, the earth is robed in new beauty, the sky glitters with a richer glory; existence assumes a grander aspect, action a higher aim, hope a nobler object, and the soul a sublimer destiny.

Such and so good is salvation in its actual enjoyment. The language of the Prophet, in the utterance of his own experience, is the language of every one whose heart thrills under a felt sense of salvation: "I will greatly rejoice in the Lord, my soul shall be joyful in my God; for he hath clothed me with the garments of salvation, he hath covered me with the robe of righteousness" (Isaiah 61:10).

II. *This good work is, secondly, described in the text as an inward or internal work.* "He which hath begun a good work *in you*." It is not a work without, but a *work within*.

When some visitors were admiring the books of the large library of a pious prelate, he replied, "One thought of devotion outweighs them all." This was a fine expression of the superior value of that which is inward and spiritual. True religion has its visible and external expressions, but they have no value unless they spring from a devout heart. Our Lord pointed out this distinction when he commended the gift of the widow's mite. Externally and visibly the gift was insignificant, but internally and spiritually it was of great value, because it expressed the devout self-sacrifice of the widow's heart.

It is a great and sublime fact that the Holy Ghost, the third Person of the blessed Trinity, dwells in the Christian. True religion is the new life with which he quickens the soul; hence religion is essentially a work within. All the issues of the Christian life must come from the heart. Redemption is a work without, a work wrought for us; but *salvation* is a good work wrought in us. If the external work of redemption is not appropriated and experienced in its internal efficacy, it is all in vain. Obvious as all this is, it is strangely misconceived and perverted. In this age of externalism, when so much thought and energy is expended upon that which is outward and material, it seems impossible to get people to understand the inwardness of true religion.

It is misconceived by many *who mistake rites and ceremonies for true religion.* It is the old mistake of the Pharisees, which our Lord so strongly rebuked, repeated age after age. They substitute the form for the power of godliness. The Scriptures everywhere teach that true religion consists in truth and purity in the inward parts. The Apostle Paul warns us that nothing outward is of any avail except as connected with a devout heart; that prophecy, alms-giving, and even martyrdom, are nothing without love. "Though I bestow all my goods to feed the poor, and though I give my body to be burned, and have not charity, it profiteth me nothing" (1 Cor. 13:3). "The kingdom of God is not meat and drink, but righteousness, and peace, and joy in the Holy Ghost" (Romans 14:17).

The inwardness of true religion is also misconceived *by those who mistake morality for religion.* Of these there are several classes. There are rationalistic theories of ethics which sever morality from religion, making religion simply a sentiment and moral conduct the essential thing. The result is to kill both morality and religion. There are some who confound the work of reformation with the work of salvation. They imagine that because they have reformed some of their external habits they are Christians. This is often a simple mistake springing from an ignorance or misconception of the truth of God. There are others (and in this age of external action it is to be feared it is a large class) who give themselves so exclusively to the activities of what is called Christian and benevolent work that they neglect to realize the inwardness of true religion in their own experience, or to develop those interior elements of spiritual life without which they are "as sounding brass or a tinkling cymbal." There are still others who seem to have the idea that morality will produce religion in their hearts; and by entering upon the practice of moral duties they indulge the expectation that this will lead to an experience of religion in their own souls.

All these classes agree in one thing—in overlooking or ignoring the inwardness of true religion; failing to realize that it is a good work wrought in them by the grace of God. They are all attempting to make the fruit good without first making the tree good, or to purify the stream without first cleansing the fountain. All these efforts to externalize religion are included in our Lord's rebuke when he said: "Now do ye Pharisees make clean the outside of the cup and the platter; but your inward part is full of ravening and wickedness. Ye fools, did not he, that made that which is without, make that which is within also?" (Luke 11: 39, 40.) Dr. James W. Alexander said, speaking to young men : "Inward, inward we must go for the true elaboration of gracious virtues. We may give ourselves too exclusively to visible activities, and have to take up the lamentation, 'They have made me keeper of vineyards, but mine own vineyard I have not kept.' It is a great moment in a man's life when he awakes to the conviction that of all the works he has to perform the greatest is within his own breast."

III. *This good work is, thirdly, described in the text as a divine work.* "Being confident of this very thing, that *he*" (that is, God) "which hath *begun* a good work in you will *perform* it until the day of Jessu Christ." It is a work which *God begins, performs* (or carries forward), and *finishes* in the day of Jesus Christ. It seems rather singular, in view of so distinct an inspired announcement, that this should be precisely the point of divergence between the two great theological systems which have divided the Church for so many ages. The question is, Who begins the work of salvation? The Arminian answers, Man himself; the first movement of the soul to God begins in the self-determining power of the human will. The Calvinist, upon the other hand, maintains that the work begins with God, and owes all its efficacy, in its origin, continuance and consummation, to divine grace. It is easy to see on which side of the question the Apostle stands, when in the text he attributes the whole work from first to last to the power of God. Indeed, if the Bible be received as the word of God, and its simple teachings be left unadulterated by the interpretations of a worldly philosophy, there can be no doubt upon this point.

That salvation is the good *work of God* follows, first, *from its internal character.* If it be a work *in us,* then he alone who made the soul can enter in to rectify and reconstruct it.

Secondly, *from the nature of the work.* It is a creation. Who can create but he who spake and it was done? It is a resurrection. Who but God can raise the dead? "You hath *he* quickened, who were dead in trespasses and sins" (Eph. 2:1). The soul thus raised is then illuminated, and who but he who commanded light to shine out of darkness can shine into our minds, "to give the light of the knowledge of the glory of God, in the face of Jesus Christ"?

Thirdly, this follows *from the Scripture descriptions of salvation as the work of God in all its issues. Its origin is in God.* "Brethren beloved of the Lord," says the Apostle, "we are bound to give thanks alway to God for you, because God hath from the beginning chosen you to salvation" (2 Thess. 2: 13, 14). *Its source is in God.* "He hath saved us, and called us with an holy calling, not according to our works, but according to his own purpose and grace, which was given us in Christ Jesus before the world began" (2 Tim. 1:9). *Its appointment is of God.* "For God hath not appointed us to wrath, but to obtain salvation by our Lord Jesus Christ" (1 Thess. 5:9). *Its execution is of God.* "It is God which worketh in you both to will and to do of his good pleasure" (Phil. 2:13). *Its grant is of God.* "This is the record, that God hath given to us eternal life, and this life is in his Son" (1 John 5:11). *Its efficacy is of God.* "He that hath wrought us for the selfsame thing is God" (2 Cor. 5:5). *Its continuance is of God.* "He is able to keep you from falling, and to present you faultless before the presence of his glory with exceeding joy" (Jude 24). Accordingly we read that the whole company of the redeemed from the earth, out of all nations and kindreds and people and tongues, as they stand before the throne and the Lamb, clothed in white robes, and with palms in their hands, cry with a loud voice: "Salvation to our God which sitteth upon the throne, and unto the Lamb" (Rev. 7:9, 10).

IV. *Again, let us notice as a fourth point that salvation is described in our text as a progressive work.* "He who hath begun a good work in you *will per-*

form it." The idea is that of a continuous, progressive performance. He will carry it on to its ultimate completion in the day of Jesus Christ.

All the works of God are progressive. The creation of the world was not instantaneous and perfect, but gradual and progressive, as the plastic hand of the Creator wrought amid chaos bringing beauty and order out of confusion, molding the world, spreading out the heavens, fashioning the stars, ordaining the sun and moon, garnishing the earth, till all stood forth in the perfection of beauty, and he pronounced it good. Revelation in like manner progressed continuously from the first dim dawn of antediluvian promise through the faint, glimmering morning of the patriarchal age and the increasing light of the prophetic period to the full-orbed, noontide effulgence of the cross of Christ.

Such also is the law of gradual and continuous progress in the work of grace; hence it is compared in the Scriptures to everything that is characterized by growth. *To the principle of vegetation,* as described by our Lord: "First the blade, then the ear, then the full corn in the ear." It is like the mustard-seed, in its first appearance the smallest, and in its ultimate development the greatest, of all trees. In like manner it is compared *to light,* growing brighter and brighter to the perfect day. *To life,* at first infantile, but the babe in Christ grows to the stature of the perfect man in Christ Jesus. *To the progress of industrial labor:* "Ye also as lively stones are built up a spiritual house" (1 Peter 2 : 5). *To the outgrowth of mechanical skill:* "He that hath wrought us for the selfsame thing is God" (2 Cor. 5 : 5).

Notice for a moment the point of this last figure. As the mechanic forges his bar and works it by a progressive process for a specific purpose, so "he that hath wrought us for the selfsame thing is God." If a piece of fine, polished, flexible steel could tell the history of the processes which have made it what it is, it would have to tell of much work done upon it, and of a great change wrought in it. It was once a dark, impure mass, scarcely to be distinguished from the stones with which it was mixed and incorporated. It would have to tell of the force that dug it out of darkness, of the blows that broke it into pieces, of the crucible in which it was closely imprisoned, of the heaps of charcoal that overlaid and of the intense fires melting the metal, changing the charcoal into a subtle gas, and forcing the new element to mix with the whole substance of the iron. It would have to tell, too, how again and again it had to feel the heavy blows of the hammer, the heat of the furious fire, the plunge into hissing, steaming water, and how it was not till after much protracted labor that the dull, heavy, brittle iron became steel, rivaling in brightness the polished silver, and in toughness the strongest cable. In like manner the Christian is wrought by God himself for his present work and future destiny. All the trials and temptations, all the sorrows and suffering, all the various changes and chances of the Christian's life, are just the blows of the hammer or the flames of the furnace that in God's providence and grace are preparing him for his future bliss. So that if a saint already bright and glittering in his inheritance of light could tell us of the processes by which he was made what he is, he would have to tell how he was dug out of the hole of the pit, of many a melting crucible, of many a plunge into the water, of many a blow of the hammer, of the fires that have been piled over and around him in the furnace of affliction, driving into his softened spirit that divine principle which has changed, not indeed the substance, but the character and qualities of his nature, giving strength instead of weakness, and infusing the grace that bends to the will of God. He would have to tell of these processes long continued and again reapplied, of fire kindled upon fire and blow succeeding blow, and that it was not until after much working and progressive refining that he was made meet for the inheritance of the saints in light.

V. Our text furnishes another invaluable point of doctrinal instruction. *This blessed, internal, divine, progressive work is here described as a work that will assuredly be completed.* Of this the Apostle gives us a double expression of his confidence. "*Being confident of this very thing,*" it is a point about which there can be no room for doubt that "he who hath begun a good work in you *will perform* it till the day of Jesus Christ."

1. *This strong confidence of the Apostle is based upon the character of God.* The simple fact that God hath begun a good work was the assurance that he would complete it. If salvation were the work of man, if either the beginning, continuance, or termination of the work depended upon ourselves, there could be no ground of certainty or confidence in the matter. But the simple fact that God has begun a good work in us leaves no room to doubt but he will carry it on to its uttermost perfection. God abandons nothing that he undertakes. There are no unfinished worlds or systems, no half-made or forsaken works of his hands. Besides this, there can be no reason why he should

begin such a work and then abandon it. It cannot be because he has no power to complete it, or because there are more enemies to be overcome than he had supposed. There is no evidence in the works of creation of any change of plan, or of his having forsaken what he began, from disappointment or disgust. He tells us himself what judgment should be formed of a builder who, having begun at great expense to erect a house, should leave it unfinished. Shall we, then, suppose that God, who hath purchased our souls with the blood of his dear Son, and has laid in our hearts the foundation of his spiritual temple, will at last leave *that* for the habitation of devils which he has been so long forming for himself? The very supposition is absurd, and its maintenance blasphemous. To suppose that God would leave unfinished a work which he has already begun is to impute weakness and imperfection to the all-perfect and ever-blessed God.

2. *While this confidence might rest with perfect security upon the basis of the divine character, it has also for its foundation the sure Word of divine promise.* These promises are of two kinds:

(1) That nothing shall destroy this work. *Not temptation,* for " God is faithful, who will not suffer you to be tempted above that ye are able; but will

with the temptation also make a way to escape that ye may be able to bear it" (1 Cor. 10: 13). *Not sin*, for "sin shall not have dominion over you" (Romans 6: 14). *Not Satan*, for the "God of all peace shall bruise Satan under your feet shortly" (Romans 16: 20). All this the Saviour comprehends in one single promise: "I give unto them eternal life; and they shall never perish, neither shall any man pluck them out of my hand" (John 10: 28).

(2) Added to these are promises of actual grace and strength, and assurances that he will carry on and perfect the work. "As thy day so shall thy strength be" (Deut. 33: 25). "The righteous also shall hold on his way, and he that hath clean hands shall be stronger and stronger" (Job 17: 9). "My grace is sufficient for thee" (2 Cor. 12: 9). "I will never leave thee, nor forsake thee" (Hebrews 13: 5). "Though the mountains depart and the hills be removed, my kindness shall not depart from thee, neither shall the covenant of my peace be removed" (Isaiah 54: 10). The Spirit of Truth, pointing to the grand inheritance beyond the grave, assures us that it is "reserved in heaven for you who are kept by the power of God through faith unto salvation" (1 Peter 1: 4 5). In view of all these assurances, we may boldly take our

stand with the Apostle upon the strength and covenant promise of God, and throw out our challenge to the world: "Who shall lay anything to the charge of God's elect?" (Romans 8: 33, 39.)

VI. *Finally, our text informs us of the time when this work will be completed.* "Will perform it until the *day of Jesus Christ*," that is, the day of his second coming, the day of his glorious appearing, when he shall come without sin unto salvation, to be admired in all his saints, but to the terror of all his enemies. "Behold, he cometh with clouds; and every eye shall see him, and all kindreds of the earth shall wail because of him" (Rev. 1: 7). This day is called *his* day, because it will be the day of his glory and triumph, when he shall see the travail of his soul and be satisfied, when all enemies shall be put under his feet, and every knee shall bow, and every tongue confess that Jesus Christ is Lord, to the glory of God the Father. Upon this day, the coronation-day of the King of Glory, when the trumpet shall sound, and all that are in their graves shall hear the call of the Son of Man and come forth, a voice, we are told, shall issue from the throne, saying, "It is done. I am Alpha and Omega, the beginning and the end" (Rev. 21: 6). It is done. Redemption is done, salvation is finished; he who began the good work in you, the

Alpha of its incipiency, is now the Omega of its completion. He hath performed it until the day of Jesus Christ.

The simple truth thus taught us is, salvation will be finished *then*—and this is the confidence of the Christian; and not till then—and this is the death of presumptuous perfectionism. But is not salvation complete at death? Nay, verily. The salvation of the soul is, for on that very day it shall be with Christ in Paradise; but not of the body, for it must repose in the grave till the Resurrection. At death, therefore, salvation is but half achieved. The soul is disenthralled, but the body, our dear mortal half, lies in the dust enduring the dishonors of the grave and the bondage of corruption. Until the day of Jesus Christ, therefore, we wait for the adoption, to wit, the redemption of the body, for it also shall be delivered from the bondage of corruption into the glorious liberty of the sons of God. Then, when the dead shall be raised incorruptible, and our happy spirits reunited to bodies now glorified, salvation will be finished. The soul and the body rewedded in a holy, happy, and indissoluble union is salvation in its uttermost perfection.

In conclusion, the whole subject resolves itself into one single inquiry: Is this good work begun in you? Without it you are of no value. Salvation is the tie that connects man with his Creator and binds him to his throne. If the tie does not exist, existence has no object. You float away a worthless atom in the universe, its proper attraction all gone, its destiny thwarted, and its whole future nothing but darkness, desolation, and death. But with this work begun in you, you are one of the precious sons of God, for whom this earth was reared and canopied with yon bright and burning blazonry. Without it you have missed the end of your creation, you are the cast-off lumber of creation, forever to be burned; but with it you are God's workmanship, and inheritors of an heirdom of glory. The efficiency is God's, the instrumentality is yours. It is yours to work, to "work out your own salvation, with fear and trembling"; it is God's to "work in you both to will and to do of his good pleasure."

INCARNATE TRUTH.

By Prof. Benjamin B. Warfield, D.D., LL.D.

"And the Word was made flesh, and dwelt among us, . . . full of . . . truth."—John 1:14.

THE obvious resemblance between the prologue to John's Gospel and the proem of Genesis is not a matter of mere phraseology and external form. As the one, in the brief compass of a few verses, paints the whole history of the creation of a universe with a vividness which makes the quickened imagination a witness of the process, so the other in still briefer compass traces the whole history of the re-creation of a dead world into newness of life. In both we are first pointed back into the depths of eternity, when only God was. In both we are bidden to look upon the chaotic darkness of lawless matter or of lawless souls, over which the brooding Spirit was yet to move. In both, as the tremendous pageants are unrolled before our eyes, we are made to see the Living God; and to see him as the Light and the Life of the world, the Destroyer of all darkness, the Author of all good. Here too, however, the Old Testament revelation is the preparation for the better to come. In it we see God as the God of power and of wisdom, the Author and Orderer of all; in this we see him as the God of goodness and mercy, the Restorer and Redeemer of the lost. Law was given through Moses; grace and truth came through Jesus Christ.

Through what a sublime sweep does the Apostle lead our panting thought as he strives to tell us who and what the Word is, and what he has done for men. He lifts the veil of time, that we may peer into the changeless abyss of eternity and see him as he is, in the mystery of his being, along with God and yet one with God—in some deep sense distinct from God, in some higher sense identical with God. Then he shows us the divine work which he has wrought in time. He is the All-Creator—"all things were made by him, and without him was not anything made that hath been made." He is the All-Illuminator—he "was the true Light that lighteth every man that cometh into the world." And now in these last days he has become the All-Redeemer—prepared for by his prophet, he came to his own, and his own received him not; but "as many as received him," without regard to race or previous preparation, "he gave to them the right to become children of God, to them that believe on his name, who were born not of blood, nor of the will of the flesh, nor of the will of man, but of God." Then the climax of this great discourse breaks on us as we are told how the Word, when he came to his own, manifested himself to flesh. It was by himself becoming flesh, and tabernacling among us, full of grace and truth. He came as Creator, as Revealer, as Redeemer: as Creator, preparing a body for his habitation; as Revealer, "trailing clouds of glory as he came"; as Redeemer, heaping grace on grace.

It is clear that it is primarily in its aspect as a revelation of God that John is here contemplating the incarnation. Accordingly, he bears his personal witness to it as such: "The Word was made flesh, and tabernacled among us, and *we beheld his glory*, a glory as of an only-begotten of the Father." Accordingly, too, he summons the prophetic witness of the forerunner. And accordingly, still further, he closes the whole with a declaration of the nature of the revelation made, and its guarantee in the relation of the incarnated Word to the Father: "No man hath seen God at any time; God only-begotten which is in the bosom of the Father, he hath declared him."

In the special verse from which we have taken

our text we perceive, then, that John is bearing his personal witness: "And the Word became flesh, and dwelt among us, and *we beheld his glory.*" He is telling us what of his own immediate knowledge he knows—testifying what he had heard, what he had seen with his eyes, what he had beheld and his hands had handled. An eye-witness to Christ's majesty, he had seen his glory and bears his willing witness to it. Nor must we fancy that he gives us merely a subjective opinion of his own, as if he were telling us only that the man Jesus was so full of grace and truth in his daily walk that he, looking upon him admiringly, had been led to conjecture that he was more than man. He testifies not to subjective opinion but to objective fact. We observe that the testimony is made up of three assertions. First, we have the fact, the objective fact, of the incarnation asserted: "And the Word was made flesh, and dwelt among us." Secondly, we have the self-evidencing glory of the incarnation asserted: "And we beheld his glory, a glory as of an only-begotten of the Father." And thirdly, we have the characteristic elements which entered into and constituted the glory which he brought from heaven with him and exhibited to men, asserted: "Full of grace and truth." Jesus Christ was incarnated love and truth. And precisely what

John witnesses is, that the Word did become flesh, and dwelt among men, full of grace and truth, and that the blaze of this his glory was manifest to every seeing eye that looked upon him.

Now it seems evident, further, that John had an especial form of the manifestation of love and truth before his mind when he wrote these words. He is thinking of the covenant God, who proclaimed himself to Moses on the mount when he descended on the cloud as "Jehovah, Jehovah, a God full of compassion, and gracious, slow to anger, and plenteous in mercy and truth." He is thinking of David's prayer, "O prepare lovingkindness and truth"; and his heart burns within him as he sees them now prepared. It is the thought of Christ's redeeming work which is filling his mind, and which leads him to sum up the revelation of the incarnation in the revelation of love and truth. Therefore he says, not "love," but "grace"—undeserved love to sinners. And in "truth" he is thinking chiefly of Christ's "faithfulness." The divine glory that rested as a nimbus on the Lord's head was compounded before all else of his ineffable love for the unlovely, of his changeless faithfulness to the unfaithful. For in Christ, God commended his love to us in that, while we were yet sinners, Christ died for us.

Nevertheless, it would be a serious error to confine the words as here used to this single implication. This is rather the culmination and climax of their meaning than the whole extent and impletion of it. Christ is not only love as manifested in grace, but as the God of love manifest in the flesh he is love itself in all its height and breadth. Not only the loftiest reaches of love, love for the undeserving, find their model in him, but all the love that is in the world finds its source and must seek its support in him. His was the love that wept at the grave of a friend and over the earthly sorrows of Jerusalem, that yearned with the bereaved mother at Nain, and took the little children into his arms to bless them; as well as the love that availed to offer himself a sacrifice for sin. In like manner, that John has especially in mind here the highest manifestations of truth—our Lord's trustiness in the great work of salvation—in no way empties the word of its lower connotations. He is still the true Light that lighteth every man that cometh into the world; and all the truth that is in the world comes from him and must seek its strength in him. "We beheld his glory," says the Apostle, "*full*"—complete, perfect—" of grace and truth." And perfection of love and truth avails for all their manifestations. This man, the man

Christ Jesus, could not act in any relation otherwise than lovingly, could not speak on any subject otherwise than truly. He is the pure fountain of love and truth.

I. We confine ourselves on the present occasion to the latter of the two characteristics here brought together. And, doing so, the first message which the declaration brings us is one so obvious that, in circumstances other than those in which we are now standing, it would seem an insult to our intelligence to direct attention to it. It is this, that since Jesus Christ our Lord, the manifested Jehovah, was as such the incarnation of truth, no statement which ever fell from his lips can have contained any admixture of error. This is John's testimony. For let us remind ourselves again that he is here bearing his witness, not to the essential truth of the divine nature incarnated in our Lord prior to its incarnation, but to the fullness of truth which dwelt in the God-man: "And the Word became flesh, and dwelt among us, and we beheld his glory, . . . full of . . . truth." More—it is the testimony of our Lord himself. "I," he declared, with his majestic and pregnant brevity, "I am the Truth." Nor dare we fancy that his plenitude of truth is exhausted in his witness to the great and eternal verities of religion, while the pettier affairs of earth and man are beyond its reach. His own norm of judgment is that only he that is faithful in the least may be trusted with the great. And it was testified of him not only that he knew whence he came and whither he went, but equally that he knew all men and needed not that any should bear witness of man, for he himself knew what was in man. He himself suspends his trustworthiness as to heavenly things upon his trustworthiness as to earthly things: "Verily, verily, I say unto you, We speak that we do know, and testify that we have seen; and ye receive not our witness. If I told you earthly things and ye believe not, how shall ye believe if I tell you heavenly things?"

Are we beating the air when we remind ourselves of such things? Would that we were! But alas! we are fallen on evil days, when we need to defend the truth of incarnate truth itself against the aspersions of even its professed friends. Oh, the unimaginable lengths to which the intellectual pride of men will carry them! Has one spun out some flimsy fancy as to the origin and composition of certain Old Testament books, which is found to clash with Jesus' testimony to their authorship and trustworthiness? We are coolly told that "as a teacher of spiritual truth sent from God and full of God he is universal," but "as a logician and critic he belongs to his times," and therefore had "a definite, restricted outfit and outlook, which could be only those of his own day and generation." "Why should he be supposed to know the science of the criticism of the Old Testament," we are asked, "which began to exist centuries after his death?" Does another cherish opinions as to the interpretation of certain Old Testament passages which will not square with the use that Christ makes of them? He tells us at once that "interpretation is essentially a scientific function, and one conditioned by the existence of scientific means, which, in relation to the Old Testament, were only imperfectly at the command of Jesus." Has another adopted preconceptions which render our Lord's dealings with the demoniacs distasteful to him? He too reminds us that the habit of ascribing disease to demoniacal influences was universal in Jesus' day, and that we can scarcely expect him to be free from the current errors of his time. Let us cut even deeper. When one desires to break out a "larger hope" for those who die impenitent than Christ's teachings will allow, he suggests that in his efforts to lead his hearers to repentance Jesus spoke habitually as a popular preacher, and far more strongly than he could have permitted himself to do had he been an exact theologian. When another burns with a zeal for moral reform which is certainly not according to knowledge, he suggests that we have reached a stage of ethical development when "new and larger perceptions of truth" have brought "new and larger perceptions of duty" than were attainable in Christ's day, and are accordingly bound to govern our lives by stricter rules than would apply to him in that darker age. Or, to sum up the whole, we have been recently told plainly that "Christ in his manhood was not the equal of Newton in mathematical knowledge," and not "the equal of Wellhausen in literary criticism," because—so we are actually told —the pursuit of such sciences requires "much exercise of mind."

Is, then, the Light that lighteth every man that cometh into the world gone out in darkness? What is left us of the Truth Indeed, who proclaims himself no more the Way and the Life than the Truth, if his testimony cannot be trusted as to the nature, origin, authority, and meaning of the Scriptures of which his own Spirit was the inspirer; as to the constitution of that spiritual world of which he is the Creator and the King; as to the nature of that future state which it is his to determine as Judge; or as to the moral life of which he is the sole author? Yet these are devout men who are propagating such teachings; and each has of course his own way of saving himself from conscious blasphemy in erecting his own thought above the thought of the God-man. The most popular way at present is to suggest that when God became man he so surrendered the attributes of divinity as that, though God, he had shrunk to the capacity of man, and, accepting the weaknesses, become subject also to the limitations of a purely human life in the world. Thus it is sought to save the veracity of the Lord at the expense of his knowledge, his truthfulness at the expense of his truth. But who can fail to see that, were this true, the sorrowing world would be left, like Mary standing weeping in the garden and crying, "They have taken away my Lord"? Where then would be Christ our Prophet? Who could assure us of his trustiness in his witness to his oneness with God, to his mission from God, to the completeness of his work for our salvation? Faith has received a serious wound, as it has been well phrased, if we are to believe that Jesus Christ could have been deceived; if we are to believe that he could—wittingly or unwittingly—deceive, faith has received its death-blow.

Let us bless the Lord, then, that he has left us little excuse for doubting in so important a matter. To the law and the testimony. Is the man Christ Jesus dramatized before us in the length and breadth of that marvelous history which fills these four Gospels, as a child of his times, limited by the intellectual outlook of his times, or rather as a teacher to his times, sent from God as no more the power of God than the wisdom of God? Is he represented to us as learning what he taught us from men, or, as he himself bore witness, from God?—"My teaching is not mine, but his that sent me;" "I am come down out of heaven," and "he that hath sent me is true"; and "the things that I have heard from him, these speak I unto the world." Did he even in his boyhood amaze the Doctors in the temple by his understanding (Luke 2:47)? Did he know even "letters," not having learned them from man (John 7:15)? Did he see Nathanael when, under the fig-tree, he bowed in secret prayer (John 1:47)? Did he know without human informant all things that ever the Samaritan woman did (John 4:29)? Did he so search the heart of man that he saw the thoughts of his enemies (Matt. 9:4); knew that one of the twelve whom he had chosen was a "devil" (John 6:70); led Peter to cry in his adoring distress, "Lord, thou knowest all things, thou knowest that I love thee" (John 20:17); and called out the testimony of John that "he knew all men, and needed not that any should bear witness concerning man, for he himself knew what was in man"

(John 2:25); as well as the testimony of all the disciples that they knew that he came from God, because "he knew all things" (John 16:30)?

But why need we go into the details that are spread from one end to the other of these Gospels? In our text itself John bears witness that the fullness of truth which dwelt in the incarnate Word so glorified all his life as to mark him out as the Son of God: "The Word became flesh, and dwelt among us, and we beheld his glory, a glory as of an only-begotten of the Father, full of truth." We surely need not fear to take our stand not only by the truthfulness but by the truth of our Lord. We surely need not shrink from, with the utmost simplicity, embracing, proclaiming, and living by his views of God and the universe, of man and the world. It was he that made the world; and without him was not anything made that hath been made. Who shall teach him how its beams were laid or how its structure has grown? It was he that revealed the Word. Who shall teach him how were written or what is intended by the words which he himself gave through his servants the prophets? It is he who is at once the Source and Standard of the moral law, and the Fount and Origin of all compassion for sinful man. Who shall teach him what it is right to do, or how it is loving to deal with the children of men? We need not fear lest we be asked to credit Jesus against the truth; we may confide wholly in him, because he is the Truth.

II. Nor let us do this timidly. Trust is never timid. Just because Jesus is the Truth, while we without reserve accept, proclaim, and live by every word which he has spoken, not fearing that after all it may prove to be false, we may with equal confidence accept, proclaim, and live by every other truth that may be made known to us, not fearing that after a while it may prove to contradict the Truth himself. Thus we may be led to the formulation of a second message which the text brings us: That since Jesus Christ our Lord, the Founder of our religion, was the very incarnation of truth, no truth can be antagonistic to the religion which he founded. John tells us that he was the true Light that lighteth every man that cometh into the world; and we may read this as meaning that as the Word of God, the great Revealer, it is he that leads man by whatever path to the attainment of whatever truth. There is, then, no truth in the world which does not come from him. It matters not through what channel it finds its struggling way into our consciousness or to our recognition, —whether our darkened eyes are enabled to catch their glimpse of it by the light of nature, as we say, by the light of reason, by the light of history, or by the light of criticism. These may be but broken lights; but they are broken lights of that one Light which lighteth every man that cometh into the world. Every fragment of truth which they reveal to us comes from him who is the Truth, and is rendered great and holy as a revelation from and of him.

We must not, then, as Christians, assume an attitude of antagonism toward the truths of reason, or the truths of philosophy, or the truths of science, or the truths of history, or the truths of criticism. As children of the light, we must be careful to keep ourselves open to every ray of light. If it is light, its source must be sought in him who is the true Light; if it is truth, it belongs of right to him who is the plenitude of truth. All natural truths must be—in varying degrees indeed, but all truly—in some sense commentaries on the supernaturally revealed truth; and by them we may be led to fuller and more accurate comprehension of it. Nature is the handiwork of God in space; history marks his pathway through time. And both nature and history are as infallible teachers as revelation itself, could we but skill to read their message aright. It is distressingly easy to misinterpret them; but their employment in the elucidation of Scripture is, in principle, closely analogous to the interpretation of one Scripture by another, though written by another human hand and at an interval of an age of time. God speaks through his instruments. Prediction interprets prediction; doctrine, doctrine; and fact, fact. Wherever a gleam of light is caught, it illuminates. The true Light, from whatsoever reflected, *lighteth*.

Let us, then, cultivate an attitude of courage as over against the investigations of the day. None should be more zealous in them than we. None should be more quick to discern truth in every field, more hospitable to receive it, more loyal to follow it whithersoever it leads. It is not for Christians to be lukewarm in regard to the investigations and discoveries of the time. Rather, the followers of the Truth Indeed can have no safety, in science or in philosophy, save in the arms of truth. It is for us, therefore, as Christians, to push investigation to the utmost; to be leaders in every science; to stand in the van of criticism; to be the first to catch in every field the voice of the Revealer of truth, who is also our Redeemer. The curse of the Church has been her apathy to truth, in which she has too often left to her enemies that study of nature and of history and philosophy, and even that investigation of her own peculiar treasures, the Scriptures of God, which should have been her chief concern. Thus she has often been forced to learn from the inadvertent or unwilling testimony of her foes the facts she has needed to protect herself from their assaults. And thus she has been led to borrow from them false theories in philosophy, science, and criticism, to make unnecessary concessions to them, and to expose herself, as they changed their positions from time to time, to unnecessary disgrace. What has the Church not suffered from her unwillingness to engage in truly scientific work! She has nothing to fear from truth; but she has everything to fear, and she has already suffered nearly everything, from ignorance. All truth belongs to us as followers of Christ, the Truth; let us at length enter into our inheritance.

III. In so speaking, we have already touched somewhat upon a third message which our text brings us: That since Christ Jesus our Lord and Master is incarnate Truth, we as his children must love the truth.

Like him, we must be so single of eye, so steadfast in purpose, so honest in word, that no guile can be found in our mouth. The philosophers have sought variously for the sanction of truth. Kant found it in the respect a man owes to the dignity of his own moral nature: the liar must despise himself because lying is partial suicide —it is the renunciation of what we are and the substitution of a feigned man in our place. Fichte found it in our sense of justice toward our fellowmen: to lie is to lead others astray and subject their freedom to our selfish ends—it is ultimately to destroy society by destroying trust among men. From each of these points of view a powerful motive to truth may be developed. It is unmanly to lie; it is unneighborly to lie. It will destroy both our self-respect and all social life. But for us as Christians no sanction can approach in power that derived from the simple fact that as Christians we are "of the Truth"; that we are not of him who when he speaketh a lie speaketh of his own, who is a liar and the father thereof, but of him who is the fullness of truth—who is light and in whom is no darkness at all. As the children of truth, truth is our essential nature; and to lie is to sin against that incarnate Truth who is also our Lord and Redeemer—in whom, we are told, no liar can have part or share.

Bare avoidance of falsehood is far, however, from fulfilling our whole duty as lovers of truth. There is a positive duty, of course, as well as this negative one beckoning us. We have already noted the impulse which should thence arise to investigation and research. If all truth is a revelation of our Lord, what zeal we should have to possess it, that we may the better know him! As children of the truth we must love the truth, every truth in its own order, and therefore especially and above all others those truths which have been revealed by God for the salvation of the world. How tenacious we should be in holding them, how persistent in propagating them, how insistent in bearing our witness to them! "To this end was I born," said our Lord himself, "and for this cause came I into the world, that I should bear witness unto the truth." And we too, as his servants, must be, each in his place, witnesses of the truth. This is the high function that has been given us as followers of Jesus: as the Father sent him into the world, so he has sent us into the world, to bear witness of the truth.

We all know in the midst of what dangers, in the midst of what deaths, those who have gone before us have fulfilled this trust. "Martyrs," we call them; and we call them such truly. For "martyrs" means "witnesses"; and they bore their witness despite cross and sword, fire and raging beasts. So constant was their witness, so undismayed, that this proverb has enshrined their eulogy for all time, that "the blood of the martyrs was the seed of the Church." They were our fathers: have we inherited their spirit? If we be Christians at all, must not we too be "martyrs," "witnesses"? must not we too steadfastly bear our witness to the truth assailed in our time? There may be no more fires lighted for our quivering flesh: are there no more temptations to a guilty silence or a weak evasion? Surely there is witness still to be borne, and we are they to bear it. The popular poet of the day sings against "the hard God served in Jerusalem," and all the world goes after him. But we—do we not know him to be the God of our salvation? the God who hath lovingly predestinated us unto the adoption of sons, through Jesus Christ, unto himself, according to the good pleasure of his will, to the praise of the glory of his grace? May God grant that in times like these, when men will not endure the sound doctrine, we may be enabled by his grace to bear unwavering witness to the glory of the Lord God Almighty, who "hath made everything for its own purpose, yea, even the wicked for the day of evil."

Need we pause further to enforce that highest form of the love of the truth, the love of the Gospel of God's grace, which braves all things for the pure joy of making known the riches of his love to fallen men? The missionary spirit is the noblest fruit of the love of truth; the missionary's simple proclamation the highest form of witness-bearing to the truth. This spirit is no stranger among you. And I am persuaded that your hearts are burning within you as you think that to you "this grace has been given, to preach unto the Gentiles the unsearchable riches of Christ, and to make all men see what is the stewardship of the mystery which from all ages hath been hid in God." You need not that I should exhort you to remember that above all else "it is required in stewards that a man be found faithful." May God grant that while you may ask in wonder, as you contemplate the work of your ministry, Who is sufficient for these things? you may be able to say, like Paul, "We are not as the many, corrupting the Word of God; but as of sincerity, but as of God, in the sight of God, speak we in Christ." May God grant that the desire which flamed in Paul may burn in you too:

> Oh could I tell ye surely would believe it!
> Oh could I only say what I have seen!
> How should I tell or how can ye receive it,
> How till He bringeth you where I have been?
>
> Give me a voice, a cry and a complaining,—
> Oh let my sound be stormy in their ears!
> Throat that would shout but cannot stay for straining,
> Eyes that would weep but cannot wait for tears.

FIRST INTERVIEW WITH THE CHRIST.

By Prof. John D. Davis, Ph.D.

"*And the two disciples heard him speak, and they followed Jesus. And Jesus turned, and beheld them following, and saith unto them, What seek ye? And they said unto him, Rabbi (which is to say, being interpreted, Master), where abidest thou? He saith unto them, Come, and ye shall see. They came therefore and saw where he abode; and they abode with him that day: it was about the tenth hour. One of the two that heard John speak, and followed him, was Andrew, Simon Peter's brother. He findeth first his own brother Simon, and saith unto him, We have found the Messiah (which is, being interpreted, Christ). He brought him unto Jesus.*"—John 1:37-42.

ONE of the two that heard John speak and followed Jesus was Andrew, who some weeks later was called to leave all and follow the Master permanently, and who later still was set apart to be an apostle. The other was John, who likewise was afterward called to permanent fellowship and then to apostleship. At least the inference that he was John is warranted by the fact that John, who alone records the event, manifests the disposition to narrate such incidents only as came, in whole or in part, under his own observation; by the fact that the minute, graphic description likewise indicates an eye-witness; by the fact that, though he mentions two men with Jesus, he leaves one unnamed —the customary modest method of John in referring to himself (21 : 2, 7).

Andrew and John could and did make a living for themselves. No shiftlessness in them. Both were fishermen, perhaps then as afterward partners in business (Luke 5 :10; Mark 1 :16). One at least had inherited from his father habits of industry, and both belonged to thrifty families, possessed some little property, and hired help in their work.

Andrew and John were, moreover, at this time, before they had felt the influence of Jesus, religious men, products of institutional religion. We must not undervalue this. We must not forget that, although Jesus had occasion to say, "Woe unto thee, Bethsaida; woe unto thee, Capernaum," he was not condemning the religion of these cities in itself, but only the spirit which animated the worshipers. The instituted religion was a power for good. With all its defects, with all its extreme views, nevertheless it maintained, amidst the darkness of a polytheistic age, the worship of the one, the true God; jealously guarded the honor of his name, as Jewish blood shed by Seleucidan and

Roman testified; taught the observance of the Sabbath by rest and public services; inculcated a lofty morality; and had lately produced characters like Simeon and Anna, Zacharias and Elizabeth, Joseph and Mary. Into this visible Church Andrew and John had been publicly admitted as infants, under its influence they had grown to manhood, and they came to Jesus with the mass of their religious beliefs correct. The minds of these men did not need to be unmade, but simply enlightened.

But more: Andrew and John were disciples of John the Baptist. They had visited the preacher at the Jordan, their eyes had been opened to sin, they had heard his call, had been baptized unto repentance, and, whatever their conduct may have been in the past, were resolved henceforth to live in newness of life and in accordance with the spirit of Israel's faith.

It is not strange that these men came to Jesus; not strange that they were the first to come. Men careless about making provision for the near future are logically and generally careless about making provision for the remote and eternal future. Men under the influence of false systems of religion, the nations of heathenism for example, are as a rule won for Christ only by the toil and patience and training of years. Men who see sin in the deed only and are content when the outside of the platter has been cleaned, men who confound respectability of life with righteousness in God's sight, do not follow Christ, for they know no need of him. Such cases are indeed not hopeless. It is a glory of Christ that he has lifted a shiftless, criminal Jerry McAuley out of vice into virtue; that his truth has led a nation of cannibals to put away cruelty and idolatry in a day; that his words pierced the self-sufficient, moral Nicodemus and won his allegiance. But this is not natural, it is exceptional. The men we expect to come to Jesus are the earnest spirits of the nation, who have been trained in the fear of the Lord from youth up, who have been taught of salvation through the Christ, who have been to Jordan and have realized and resolved that the ax must be laid to the root of the tree, that sin must be destroyed in the heart. For such, as it was for Andrew and John, it is only a step to Jesus, only a step to a life-long fellowship with the Master.

May we not pause here to consider what this means with reference to our methods of work? Is it wise for us to seek to carry the good news of salvation post-haste and as mere heralds through the world? Or shall the Christian Church, to whose trust has been committed the Gospel, in its work of transmission and extension found and foster churches, establish schools, gather in the children, train them in the maxims of wisdom, teach them the law of God and his holy fear, seek to impress upon them the guilt and loathsomeness of sin, show them that its roots are in the heart, and point them to the Christ as prophet, priest, and king? Success does not always attend such efforts; but history from the time of John the Baptist until now declares that that is the true way. As we scatter to all parts of the earth on the Master's business, let us remember this. To whatever part of this comprehensive work you may be called, whether teaching rudiments or unfolding the glory of Christ to eager, anxious souls, remember that your work is a necessary part of the great whole, and do it for Christ's sake. There is a difference of privilege, but the same work. Aim to prepare Andrews and Johns.

Jesus turned, beheld the two men following, and said unto them, "What seek ye?" They said unto him, "Rabbi, we seek to know where thou abidest." He said unto them, "Come, and ye shall see." They came, saw where he abode, and tarried with him that day. He had just come from the wilderness victor over temptation, triumphant in faith and purpose. His act was an intentional revelation, the first revelation of his public ministry.

It showed to those men the possibility of fellowship with the Christ. How gracious he was! Regarded with awe by their teacher the Baptist, declared by him to be the God-chosen King, the ardently desired Messiah, they felt him to be far above them. They had followed at a distance respectfully, timidly; venturing only to come near enough to learn where he dwelt. He, however, noticed them, trusted them, did honor to their manhood, granted their request to know where he dwelt by inviting them to his abiding-place, walked side by side with them thither, and talked with them by the way. John the Baptist had spoken glorious things about the Great Unknown who stood in their midst, but the half had not been told. Suddenly a great light had shined upon them. The Christ was full of grace.

But not only did the Christ's attitude reveal graciousness, it showed his fearless openness. He was ready to be seen as he was: to take them at once, without preparation, and show them his plain lodgings, probably a booth; to let them study his manner of life, to examine him himself. He was like the neighboring river in which they had been baptized, like the huge mountains behind which the declining sun was about to set, like the deep blue sky overhead—full of mystery, but hiding nothing. He that had eyes to see and ears to hear, a mind to think and a heart to feel, might study and know who he is. No wonder that afterward one of these two men who followed Jesus described him as one whom he had seen with his eyes, whom he had heard, whom his hands had handled—full of grace and truth. Jesus did nothing secretly; he ever taught openly in the Temple; he performed his mighty works indifferently where.

Jesus had revealed to Andrew and John the possibility of intimate fellowship with him. And "they abode with him that day." Afterward Andrew sought out his brother Simon and said unto him, "We have found the Messiah." Behold the effect of intercourse with Jesus. Their brief interview with Jesus had wrought in them the conviction that he was the Christ. "We have found the Messiah."

And yet there was apparently nothing extraordinary in that interview. Jesus certainly wrought no miracle; for that was delayed, as we know, until the marriage at Cana, and then called forth a new faith in these men. There was no miracle; and, we judge, not even a revelation of that superhuman knowledge which he manifested a day or so later when he said to Nathanael, "Before that Philip called thee, when thou wast under the fig tree, I saw thee." The Apostle John in narrating the first meeting of himself and Andrew with Jesus records it as a simple interview; memorable, not by mighty deeds, but by its effects upon two lives.

It was, moreover, the same Jesus that had mingled with men for thirty years. Why, then, should he who was merely respected in Nazareth so mightily impress these men now? In part, because while a youth in his father's house he had not been pointed out to men as the Messiah. The story of his birth and of his presentation in the Temple belonged to the privacy of the family. The friends of the Baptist's parents knew of Zacharias' dumbness, and of his fervent declaration, when his tongue was loosed, that the son who had just been born to him should be the forerunner of the Messiah; but there is no reason to suppose that the kindred of the Baptist knew anything connected with the birth of Jesus. It is true also that the shepherds had looked upon the child, and that wise men from the east had come to Herod asking where he should be born that was to be King of the Jews. But the shepherds returned to their work in the fields, the wise men had quietly left the country, and Joseph had taken Mary and the young child into Egypt. Herod's excitement occasioned by the visit of the Magi, leading to the convocation of the doctors of the law to declare unto him where the Christ should be born and reflecting itself in anxiety throughout the city as to what course the freak would take, had been allayed when Herod sent armed men to Bethlehem to slay all the babes of two years and under. When after two years the parents of Jesus again settled in Nazareth, it was merely noised abroad that the carpenter and his wife had come back from Egypt and a first-born child with them.

When Jesus began to be about thirty years of age, there were apparently but two persons alive who were acquainted with his early history, Mary and John the Baptist; and these two believed on him. John had probably heard from his mother regarding his cousin, but he had refrained from pointing him out until authorized. Mary treasured the events connected with the infant Jesus and pondered them in her heart. She alone was left as witness, and it is doubtless due chiefly to the testimony of this woman that we owe our knowledge of the early life of the Master. Jesus had not affected his fellow-townsmen as he was now affecting the two fishermen, partly because his title was unproclaimed. His beautiful character had indeed been recognized; he grew in favor with God and man. His insight into the Scriptures as early as his twelfth year was acknowledged by the doctors of the law at Jerusalem; and there is some reason to suppose that he had been accepted by the Nazarenes as a reader of the Word of God in their synagogue. He was indeed a light; but he was a light shining in darkness, the darkness comprehending it not.

But again, while in Nazareth not only had he been unproclaimed, he had hidden his light; now his hour had come. At Jordan he had been anointed by the Spirit for the work; in the wilderness he had been chastened by temptation, and had emerged consecrated to his mission; from the Baptist he had received official announcement. Henceforth he is able and willing to reveal himself and his doctrine fully and freely to men. Andrew and John catch the first glimpse of that revelation, are the first to see the effects of that conflict and feel the influence of the ennobled soul.

But even that was not enough to account for the mighty impression the Christ made upon those two friends; for when Jesus later returned to Nazareth and offered himself to his countrymen, they led him to the brow of the hill upon which their city was built, and would have cast him headlong over the brink. Testimony and character impressed Pilate also; but they did not make the Roman a follower

FIRST INTERVIEW WITH THE CHRIST. 125

of the Christ. Since his day testimony and character have impressed thousands, so that with Rousseau they confess that the life and death of Jesus are those of a God; and yet they refuse to bow in loyal allegiance to him.

In the case of Andrew and John the impression was made upon men prepared. The two friends had already turned from sin to God. The contrite heart joyfully receives the approved Christ; and therefore again we say, Aim to prepare men for Christ by leading them to repentance. In the early days of this century in western Pennsylvania the mighty servants of God who labored in that then wilderness followed this method. Gathering the people together in Nature's temples, holding what many suppose to be the first camp-meetings, day after day they preached the law, the heart's guilt, the wrath of God, until the audience cast themselves prostrate on the ground undone. Then, and not till then, was the gracious Saviour held up, sinners believed and arose, and a sturdy, godly generation sprang into being. From the days of John the Baptist until now it is in men awake and repentant that testimony to the Christ confirmed by his character is effectual.

And now let us ask what there was in this special interview with Jesus that convinced these men that he was the Christ. As already noticed, there was no miracle; so far as known, no display of superhuman knowledge. There was, however, the man—his personality, his aspect. There was the manner—supreme grace warming the heart, awakening affection; frank openness begetting confidence. There was the talk—as of one with authority, and not as the scribes, at which long before the doctors in the Temple had marveled; talk of which the graciousness later at Nazareth awakened the wonder of his fellow-citizens; talk which more than once by its unanswerable logic and heart-searching power silenced the wily questioner; talk which disarmed the opposition of men sent to lay hands on him, and called forth from them the declaration, "Never man spake as this man"; talk which, on the way to Emmaus, the speaker unrecognized, caused the hearts of two downcast disciples to burn within them.

It was these things, the man, the manner, the converse, which convinced Andrew and John that they had found the Messiah; yea more, which wrought in them the belief that an interview with Jesus would convince other men also: for Andrew sought his brother, saying, "We have found the Messiah," and brought him to Jesus; and Philip told Nathanael that they had found him of whom

Moses in the law and the prophets did speak, Jesus of Nazareth; and to the rejoinder, "Can any good thing come out of Nazareth?" replied, "Come and see."

And in these elements there is evidence of Messiahship of great convincing power.

1. It is impossible to close the eyes to the fact that, as promised in the Mosaic law, a masterful Prophet had arisen like unto Moses; whose right to acknowledgment stood attested, for unquestionably he spake according to the law and the testimony.

2. Not only was a Prophet undoubtedly before them, they recognized in him the predicted character also of the servant of the Lord. In his graciousness and sympathy they read the story, "Behold my servant, whom I uphold; my chosen, in whom my soul delighteth. . . . He shall not cry, nor lift up, nor cause his voice to be heard in the street. A bruised reed shall he not break, and the smoking flax shall he not quench." "He hath sent me to bind up the broken-hearted, to proclaim liberty to the captives, and the opening of the prison to them that are bound."

Brethren, it will be your privilege, as it was the privilege of Peter and Paul, to prove from the Scriptures of the Old Testament that Jesus is the veritable, long-promised Christ. The temptation is too often yielded to, to build the argument solely on minute predictions, to cite those passages only which refer, and which have ever been understood by the Jews to refer, to the place of the Christ's birth and to other incidents of his history. We would utter no word of condemnation against such an argument when made with scholarly discrimination and adequate knowledge. It subserves one purpose of prophecy; it is authorized by the New Testament; it is a mighty weapon for attack and defense; it satisfies the craving for definite proof. But do not stop with this argument, neglecting the weightier matter. Go to the valley of the Jordan and learn from the two disciples who first followed Jesus that before the events of his life had been enacted, before there were definite incidents to which minute predictions in any number could be applied, there was enough in Jesus to convince that the fulfillment of prophecy was there. Jesus in himself and Jesus during the Christian era has realized the predicted character, and that is the great argument from prophecy.

3. There was perhaps a third element which corroborated their faith. His was a character in contrast to their own. We cannot tell how clear to their minds at this interview was the wide differ-

ence between them and the Master. But if their senses were acute enough to discern it, the contrast convinced. I believe that a man whose eyes are open to the subtle nature, the guilt and the loathsomeness of sin; a man who in grief and hatred thereof has turned from it unto God; who as he contends with evil, struggles with adversity, and journeys through mysterious darkness, keeps his eyes fixed on Jesus in like but yet fiercer conflict, and finds Jesus, in contrast with himself, ever the strong, patient, uncomplaining, trustful, obedient, sinless Son of the heavenly Father—gazing thus with senses exercised and keen, cannot fail to recognize in Jesus, and in this teeming world in Jesus alone, the King. The figure stands solitary in earth's history who is glorious in holiness.

There stood a mighty Prophet; there was the predicted character of the Lord's Servant; there was a peerless One. The good news proclaimed by John the Baptist was true. The Christ had indeed come.

RELIGION IN COLLEGE.*

BY PRESIDENT FRANCIS L. PATTON, D.D., LL.D.

"*I write unto you, young men.*"—1. JOHN 2:13.

IF any one should say that it is intrinsically harder for men to be religious than women, I do not know that I should dispute the proposition. I certainly should not do it without making allowance for the special temptations to which men are subject, the irreligious atmospheres into which they are thrown, and the many influences unfriendly to religion which seem to beset husbands, sons and brothers, of which wives and mothers and sisters are in a measure at least happily ignorant. And so I can understand the special interest with which an audience of men is regarded, and the special ground for gratitude that there is when in some time of religious interest the claims of the Gospel take hold of men.

There is good reason, too, for the particular interest that is felt in young men, and above all,

* Preached at the opening of the college year.

the religious life of young men. For they seem to carry with them the world's fortunes. The passing generation sees the promise of its own immortality in the rich new life of these young men. Their life is all before them. They have no past. Their future is, so to speak, a matter of their own making. We commit the world of the future to their senses; the bright electric nights to their vision; the new discoveries of science to their admiration. "We shall not live to see the day, but you will," we are accustomed to say, and so we use the younger generation to give ourselves an artificial longevity. There is a peculiar sympathy which a young man awakens in us—awakens, I mean, especially in men. We understand him. How much of our life he is repeating! How in all he does he seems to be plagiarizing from the book of our own memory! His hopes, his ambitions, his dreams, his enthusiasms, sometimes his magnified estimate of himself and his disregard of the wisdom of his elders— have we not experienced it all? His follies, too, and his blunders, his non-malicious wrong-doing, sometimes even his sins—did we not go before him? Ah then, unless we are selfish, unless we are unwilling that others shall excel us—here is the secret of our anxiety, of our interest in the welfare of these young lives. It is the contrast between ourselves conditioned, handicapped by age, by habit, by the momentum we have gathered in the rush down the stream, and these young men with their future before them and in their own hands that draws us to them. If we had our lives to live over again, we say, we should act differently. We should study this and not neglect that. But now it is too late, and we must make the best of such undisciplined or ill-disciplined powers as we have. But these young men we think can avoid these mistakes; and we would fain, if they would let us act as pilot for them, steer them clear of the rocks on which our own barks were well-nigh shipwrecked years ago. Oh, how wise and good the race would be if wisdom were cumulative, and we the heirs of all the ages had come into possession of an unwasted inheritance!

And when to youth we add the advantage of intellectual culture we magnify the interest felt in those who possess them both. For it needs no prophet to see in them the men who for good or ill will shape the history of the next generation. Men fail sometimes to fulfill the promise of their youth. They grow sick or lose heart, or succumb to luxury, or fall into evil habits; but for all that the world's hope and the world's future are with the educated young men of to-day.

The college graduate is of more importance, I dare say, than the undergraduate. It is fair to suppose that he is a larger factor in the great world's life. Indeed, it is in order to get ready for that great world that we come to college; and so because the graduate has gone out from us we must not on that account hold him in light esteem. But it is the undergraduate who has special interest in our eyes. There are good reasons for this. The college world is *sui generis*. College life changes a man the moment he begins to live it. Men come hither from all parts of the country; they represent different habits of thought, states of society, and modes of existence. And when they are here they preserve an individuality that saves them from any loss of identity in their intercourse with one another. They can be separated into groups according to several principles of division, and these groups have appropriate designations in our rich academic vernacular. But to the outside world they all look alike, they think alike, they talk alike, they are imbued with the same spirit and seem to possess a common life. They have their burning questions and their organs of opinion. They have their own vocabulary and, to a certain extent, their own code of ethics.

There are good and bad features in this segregated academic life. It would be better on some accounts if we were in closer sympathy with the every-day life of the world. But on the other hand there is something elevating in the ideas that bring about this state of things. A man need not study hard in order to keep his academic standing, but the studious men give college life its character. And there is that in intellectual work that separates a man from the world. Bring men of intellectual tastes together and you of necessity establish an intellectual caste. You create a community that loves refinement and that protests against all that is sordid and vulgarizing.

I am expressing myself, therefore, in the tamest words when I say that no audience can excite my interest like the one that faces me to-day. You are standing on the threshold of manhood or have barely crossed it. You have had your first glimpses of the new world of thought and knowledge that is open to your exploration. You have begun to feel your own power and to try your strength in grappling with the great questions of life and destiny. Your thoughts have not yet dug for themselves the grooves which make the thinking of some people easy by making it narrow and repetitious. You have hardly decided yet what channels your energies shall run in, and you like to keep it still an open question what your profession shall be, lest you come prematurely into bondage to a career. You are at the transition stage, perhaps, in your religious life, when the faith of childhood is hardening into reasoned conviction, or when perhaps you fear a schism between your reason and your heart. And in the short life of an academic generation you will go out from this unique undergraduate existence into the larger life of the world, helped, it may be—God forbid that you should be hindered—in your dealings with these great questions by what you hear from us who meanwhile are your official guides. I ask no greater privilege on earth than that I may be able from time to time to speak in a worthy, helpful way from this pulpit to you and to those who, after you, shall occupy these pews.

My text does not shut me up to any given line of thought, but you will already have gathered that my remarks will be based upon the relations of religion to college life. Let me have your attention, then, while I say a few words in reference to two questions: 1. How religion should affect your college life. 2. How college life should affect your religion.

I. I take it for granted that, in a certain sense at least, most of you are religious men. Many of you are avowedly so. You come for the most part from religious homes. You are men of religious convictions, even though you may have given no formal expression to your convictions. You have not discarded the faith in which you were trained, though possibly you have not made any acknowledgment of it. You will so far admit the claims of the Gospel as to recognize your obligations to conform to its teaching, however much in the case of some of you your lives may contradict that teaching.

How should the Gospel, as you have been taught it, affect your college career? How should it operate upon that individual and corporate life of which we are bound to take cognizance in the administration of college affairs?

The day has gone by when it was necessary to show that a man might be a Christian and at the same time enjoy life. The Christian who thinks that depression of spirits is a sign of piety belongs to an extinct type. When it is urged, therefore, that athletic sports foster a manly spirit and develop healthy tissue; when it is said that the element of emulation is necessary to give them zest; and when without undue waste of time, without the sacrifice—as has confessedly been the case in more than one instance—of an entire session's work

in the class-room, when, without contributing to
the gambling habit—which has already become a
national curse—the representatives of leading colleges engage in honorable and gentlemanly contests for supremacy; I do not feel that there is
in all this any necessary compromise of Christian
principle, and it would never occur to me to repent at my leisure of any impulsive enthusiasm that
I may have evinced. There is no reason why a man
should forfeit his manliness by being a Christian.
He should cultivate a gentle spirit, and the passive
virtues have a high place among the Christian
graces. With the etiquette, with the unwritten
code of honor existing among undergraduates
which controls so much of their relation to one
another and to college authorities, I have a great
deal of sympathy; though I think that some good
principles are allowed too wide a range of application. A man is not called upon—at least in ordinary circumstances—to be a tale-bearer or a spy
even in the interests of religion. I have no difficulty in making pretty large concessions to undergraduate sentiment in more things than one. It
would be hard for you to make demands with respect to the inviolability of personality and the
rights of manhood that I am not prepared to grant.
You sustain relations to the governing body of this

college that give rise to perplexing problems and that involve difficulties that you hardly appreciate. But I would rather bear with the difficulties than take an unbidden step across the threshold of your inner life. The incredulous look, the suggestion that impeaches your motive, the inquiry that needlessly assails the very citadel of your manhood, you have a right to be aggrieved at. There is no fundamental difference of sentiment between professors and students in this college so far as these matters are concerned, though it is more than likely there may be a difference of emphasis. You would very properly have us remember that you are men. We, on the other hand, cannot well forget that you are young men. That is the whole of it. And it should not be a matter of offense if, when I speak of the excellences of your life, I call your attention to some of its limitations.

When you and I are old enough we shall be sedate perhaps, calm, self-contained, judicial. Now, however, our friends must bear with us; and if we are only ingenuous, kind-hearted, and responsive to affectionate treatment, they must give us credit for it; and we must not take it ill if they tell us plainly that we are impulsive, hot-headed, swayed by feeling, and a trifle inconsiderate. I dare say we are. But if we are Christians, and we profess to make practical use of Christian principles, we should study to conform our conduct to these principles. It will not do for us to fall back upon our Christian faith as an atonement for our unchristian practice.

There are a great many ways in which I might profitably apply Christian principle to college life. I think the lack of conscientiousness is perhaps a serious matter with all of us. Many a man, I am sure, would find a spur to diligence in study if he would seriously interrogate his conscience as to the use of his own time and his father's money during his undergraduate days. Many a man would be saved from the indiscretions incident to the young gregarious life of college students if he would take time to reflect upon his personal accountability to God. And here I am reminded of one or two at least of the faults that are characteristic of your class which I think your religion ought to enable you to redress.

We must rely upon personal religion to correct the evil tendency of the gregarious habit in college students by the assertion of individual responsibility. There is a tendency for the individual to lose himself in the organism that he belongs to. That there is a good side to this I can very readily allow. It saves a man from conceit, it is a check upon the egotism that intellectual life is so apt to foster, it is a lesson in the great art of bearing one another's burdens, it is an illustration of the truth that we are members one of another—when a student is ready to sink personal advantage for the honor of his class, or when all make common cause in the interest of one. We should lose much if we did not have the instinct that leads us to realize a corporate life. The Church is founded upon this idea. When one member suffers all the members suffer with it. Society itself presupposes it. And when, in our selfishness, in our greed of distinction or of gain, in our pride of intellect and self-sufficiency, we isolate ourselves, or are cut off from fellowship by the tacit mandate of our fellows, we are working for the disintegration of social life. I love the principle that lies at the bottom of corporate undergraduate class-sentiment. It is to a great extent a peculiarity of American colleges. It is something that our system of prizes offered in competition has so far not superseded. And much as I believe in giving honor where honor is due, and holding out inducements for high intellectual attainment, I should be sorry if a spirit of individualism, of jealous and querulous antagonism, should ever grow up among the undergraduates of our colleges, that would make it necessary for Professor

Bryce to qualify the generous words which he uses in his recent book on the American Commonwealth, when, after speaking of some of the characteristics of the American University, he says: "The other merit is that the love of knowledge and truth is not, among the better minds, vulgarized by being made the slave of competition and of the passion for quick and conspicuous success. An American student is not induced by his university to think less of the intrinsic value of what he is learning than of how far it will pay in an examination, nor does he regard his ablest fellow-students as his rivals over a difficult course for high stakes, rivals whose speed and strength he must be constantly comparing with his own." There is, however, a bad side to this corporate or class sentiment, and it is that under the operation of it a man will let his conscience sleep and make the corporate sentiment do her work. You do not like to seem peculiar; you do not care to be over-righteous or over-wise. You do not think that there can be much harm in what all the rest approve. And so, true to your gregarious instincts, true to that subtle law of your nature that affirms the solidarity of social life, you force conscience to abdicate when she stands up for the sovereignty of the individual, and you follow the multitude to do evil. I do not know a more needed lesson among college men than that concerning the sacredness of the individual conscience. There is a great deal in the inspiration of a common cause; but there is a limit to a man's obligation to sacrifice his personality even in a good cause. Let no man invade your self-hood. Do not put your personality into a common fund. Do not tamper with the autonomy of your own conscience by putting it under the control of an organization. I look upon it as one of the most disastrous things in our moral life to-day that we are so under the tyranny of public sentiment, so conditioned by the fear of what other people will say or think, that we do not give our conscience a fair chance, and in consequence are beginning to lose the sense of face-to-face accountability to God. If this be so, even with regard to things that at least can be said to have good motives behind them, how much more are we to be blamed when we allow ourselves to tolerate or take part in proceedings that we would have no thought of defending, except on the plea that they all do it.

We must also rely upon the religious convictions of Christian men to correct a false doctrine of relativity that prevails among college students. Theoretically we are agreed: right is right; wrong is wrong; always, everywhere. Practically, it is otherwise. There is one standard for the individual, another for the organization. Let us not deal with this question by way of excessive refinement. Cases do differ, and where conduct is considered, time, place, and circumstances must be considered. There is no rudeness offered by a slap on the shoulder where that is a recognized mode of salutation among comrades. Whether entering your house without knocking is an insult or only a sign of friendship depends on what our relations are. Whether a given act is an injury depends on how it is taken: *Volenti non fit injuria:* those old Romans put a great deal of sense into their maxims. And yet there is an abuse of this idea of relativity in morals that calls for very serious consideration. If you say that it goes everywhere and affects Christians generally, I am sorry to admit that this is true. Some men do in Europe what they will not do at home. Some are dishonest and untruthful in the minor matters and conventionalities of life, who in more serious things are very scrupulous and honest. This, however, is no excuse for that phase of relativity with which we are made familiar in college morals according to which a freshman's room is an exception to the law that a man's house is his castle; according to which it is wrong to lie, but right to deceive a professor; according to which it is wrong to steal, but right to take aids to reflection into an examination hall.

Let me not be understood as making a sweeping allegation in what I say. I am aware of the high moral tone that prevails in this college; and that the matters referred to are of comparatively infrequent occurrence, and that when they do occur it is but rarely that they imply any fixed determination of character. In respect to some of these matters there is a growing sentiment among undergraduates that will soon, I hope, become so strong as to supersede both law and police; for I have more confidence in the Christian conscience than I have in any other agency. Our hope of reforming college morals lies in addressing the conscience. It is only as laws reach the conscience that they have much practical value. Therefore, when they are oppressive and suggest injustice, they should be modified in the interest of morality.

We must look, then, to the religious men of the college to exert positive influence in the creation of a proper public sentiment. They are numerous enough, they are possessed of sufficient weight of character, and their influential position in the great centers of undergraduate influence is great enough, to enable them to control sentiment; and when it is understood that undergraduate sentiment will not tolerate the presence of the man who habitually defies the law of God and of good manners, the era of academic freedom will dawn.

I appeal, therefore, to your Christian sentiments and your religious convictions, gentlemen, as the basis, and the only basis upon which we can proceed, toward the abolition of multitudinous laws, toward the repeal of regulations that seem in the judgment of some to be out of keeping with the life of full-grown men.

I think there are some things that a man's manliness should do for him, and that certainly his religion should do for him. It should give him such a conscientious desire to receive instruction that it would not be necessary to keep a double-entry account of his attendance in the class-room, with a debit to absence and a credit to excuse; it should inspire even a somewhat feeble person with strength to stand on his feet during the singing of a morning hymn; and it should furnish a motive for a proper use of time in the acquisition of knowledge that would make it a superfluous labor for professors to find mathematical equivalents in whole numbers and fractions of an examination paper that represents in too many cases the indolence of a term and the industry of the night before.

You complain of bondage and sigh for freedom.

I sympathize with you. I am on your side. But the matter is in your own hands. And when in reference to those things that now make laws a necessity there shall have come about that change of sentiment that plainly says, "When I was a child I thought as a child, I spake as a child, I understood as a child, but when I became a man I put away childish things"—then, too, will come the freedom that you seek; for the law will cease to be statute by being transformed into life, and it will thenceforth be the perfect law of liberty.

In what I have been saying I have had special reference to the bearing of your religious profession upon your corporate life as a student-body and upon the relation which you sustain as a body of undergraduates to the college authorities. I have not said anything about the influence which your religion should exert in keeping you from spiritual harm: and one would think that if Christian convictions are worth anything they should enable you to say "No" to temptation, and resist solicitations to vice. It is to be feared, however, that there is a great deal of weak religion in the world, and I am afraid that matters are not improved by the unmanly way in which we sometimes talk upon the subject. It is a pity that we accustom ourselves to this effeminate mode of regarding Christian faith: when instead of being a shield which protects us from assaults, instead of being a stout club with which we knock temptation on the head, instead of being a sword wherewith we slay our spiritual enemies, it is regarded rather as a very weak companion that we must nurse tenderly and that cannot go out at night. I wish there were more robust piety in the world and less of the sickly kind. There would then be less occasion for the solicitude that parents now feel regarding the religious health of their sons who come to college. I must, however, respect this solicitude.

II. Having, therefore, spoken in the first place on the question, How religion should affect your college life, I must now speak on the question, How college life should affect your religion. Many an anxious parent is raising this question to-day. He knows that in this seat of learning his son will have many advantages of an intellectual kind, but he wonders whether he will not also be exposed to a great many temptations, and whether in his gain of learning he may not lose his soul. There can be no doubt that a college man has to face temptations. We do our best to keep immoral influences out of the college, and I believe in dealing with these influences with a strong hand. When common fame accuses a man of exerting a corrupting influence in the college, I want no maxims from the common law to stand in the way of college purity. Do not quote under such circumstances the doctrine of second jeopardy, or say that the law looks *in favorem vitae.* Do not tell me that a man is innocent until he is found to be guilty, or suppose that the provisions of the criminal suit will apply to college procedure. There are times when a man should be held guilty until he is found innocent, and when it is for him to vindicate himself and not for us to convict him.

But when we have done our best, it will be impossible for us to guarantee those who come here against temptations. Adolescence has its perils, and I do not know that a man would escape them if he remained at home. Parents sometimes speak of the special temptations of college life: as though there were no temptations in business; as though clerks in banks and in brokers' offices were all the time under holy influences; as though the philosophers of Wall Street were somehow in closer touch with the ten commandments. I suppose that men in shops and on farms have to face temptation. A man may shun his kind, but he cannot shun himself. He may avoid all company but his own, and sometimes that is the worst.

There are perils to morals, and there are perils

to faith in connection with a college life—probably no greater in college than elsewhere. Men sometimes make sad failures in college. They leave home with good intentions and noble purpose, but are weak-willed and wanting in stability, form bad companionships, and are led into corrupting practices. They come from homes where they have been kept under constant watch and have had to give strict account of their time, and find even the limited freedom allowed them here too much for them: they become indolent and lose relish for study. They are thrown into a larger companionship than they had ever known before, and when they find that their capacity for leadership in all that is daring and in contravention of established law has made them popular, their scholarly ambitions die a very easy death.

I fear lest there may be some of you who are making these mistakes, and I am sorry for you; but I am more sorry for your fathers and mothers who sent you here, and whose agony of disappointment I think no one can well understand who has not had boys of his own. And yet a man who succumbs to temptation in college would in all probability fare no better elsewhere. Sooner or later a man must learn to take care of himself. He must come into possession of his freedom, and it is no small part of a good education to prepare a man in the best manner for the use of that freedom. I do not think that it is wise to perpetuate in college the methods of the preparatory school. Rules there must be, but they should be as few and simple as possible. Requirements of attendance there should be, and a proper method of enforcing them, but they should be in keeping with the advancing years, the maturing powers, and the approaching manhood of those to whom they apply. And it seems to me that it is one of the special features of your life here that you come into possession of that freedom of thought and action that you rightly prize as one of the chief attributes of your manhood, under the best conditions. You are invested with the franchises of manhood in a time and way that suggest personal responsibility; and so that instead of opening a door for self-indulgence, they become a factor in your moral education. I do not think that the college student feels on his twenty-first birthday an impulse to throw off the yoke of parental authority; I am inclined to suppose that he is only made the more conscious by the occasion that he must soon take the responsibility of his future in his own keeping. You are living under conditions best fitted to make you feel what Dr. Chalmers called the expulsive power of a new affection. You are dealing with serious problems. You are reading the best books. Your employments are elevating. You are handling great questions in history, morals, economics, politics; and whether these questions are treated under distinctively religious conceptions or not, they suggest religious ideas, for they suggest the idea of the fitting, the best, the right, the true. You are not simply studying facts. You are not asking merely what is, but what ought to be. You are forming ideals, and when you are doing that you are on the border-land of religion. It is not religious prejudice, it is sound philosophy that Principal Shairp gives utterance to when he says that religion is the goal of culture.

A man's studies should have a moral as well as an intellectual influence upon him. Physics should make him more truthful, Astronomy more reverent, Literature more genial, Social Science more benevolent, Philosophy more believing. The law of the Lord is perfect. Nature teaches that as well as Scripture. The star keeps its appointment with the observer, and the belated Frenchman only revealed his vanity and his ignorance when he asked the astronomer to *encore* the eclipse. And besides this indirect religious influence that serious study in all lines is fitted to exert, there is in this college especially, and I trust there always will be, a body of men who, however strong they may be in their departments, and however enthusiastic they may be in the prosecution of them, are not ashamed to say: "I believe in God the Father Almighty, the Maker of heaven and earth, and in Jesus Christ, his only Son." To this Christian influence many a man in the years to come will express obligation for the perpetuation of his religious faith. Many a man will say when asked what saved him from skepticism, in words that bear a different meaning from that which he who wrote them intended:

> "For rigorous teachers seized my youth
> And purged its faith and trimmed its fire,
> Showed me the high white Star of Truth,
> There bade me gaze and there aspire."

There are, as I have already said, perils of faith as well as perils of morals in connection with a career in college. This is unavoidable. The possibility of religious doubt can be avoided only by avoiding religious questions altogether; and religious questions can be avoided only by deliberately choosing a life of stupidity and ignorance. All questions are at bottom religious questions; all inquiries have religious implications. Back of physics lie metaphysics. Behind the facts of history lies the philosophy of history. Economic questions raise ethical problems, and our view of ethical problems will depend very much upon whether we believe in God. College men have also among them those who are under strong impulse to antagonize established beliefs, or who seek to show originality by constructing a universe of their own. There are conceited men who show their intellectual pride by treating religious faith with scorn; and weak-minded men who come under the spell of a favorite author and cannot admire his style without imbibing his views. And there are besides those who feel honestly, earnestly, interested in knowing for themselves the reasons for the faith in which they were trained. They will not consent to hold a merely traditional creed, and, though it cost them many a struggle, are determined to reach bedrock before they consent to build the house of faith.

The man of this sort—I have great respect for him—is very apt to be an educated man:

> "Perplexed in faith, but pure in deeds,
>   At last he beat his music out;
>   There lives more faith in honest doubt,
> Believe me, than in half the creeds.
>
> "He fought his doubts and gathered strength;
>   He would not make his judgment blind,
>   He faced the specters of the mind
> And laid them; thus he came, at length,
>   To find a stronger faith his own."

And yet when we remember how skepticism parades itself in our newspapers, publishes itself in our magazines, lectures to us from the rostrum, and assails our ears in the street-car; when we see the facility with which the charlatan poses as a philosopher, and how a witty infidel can produce the impression of being the sum of all wisdom, we need not suppose that the college student is exposed to any special temptations. On the contrary, the very conditions under which he carries on his work are favorable to the conservation of his religious faith.

You have learned very little, my friends, if you have not already learned that the kings of thought—those, that is to say, who reign by divine right—are very different from those who have been crowned kings by an undiscriminating public. Real culture is aristocratic; and you will naturally be legitimists in your intellectual partisanships. You will not let Tyndall speak as your authority in physics, nor regard Haeckel as infallible in biology, and you will not credit Herbert Spencer with the omniscience that his ambitious system would seem to imply. Your training has taught you that a man does not acquire a right to speak with authority on all subjects because he has made one subject his own. You know the limits of demonstrative certainty, and you know, as the common mind does not know, that men are making demands for a kind and a degree of proof for historic Christianity that, applied to other subjects, would throw the whole business of investigation into hopeless bankruptcy. You will not raise foolish questions regarding the trustworthiness of the entire text of Scripture when you are told that the best manuscripts do not support the statement in the gospel about the angel at the pool of Bethesda; for you have no doubt about Virgil's poem, though the lines beginning, "*Ille ego qui quondam*," etc., that in the old editions stood at the opening of the Æneid, are now understood to be spurious. You will not wonder whether your New Testament is the genuine product of the writers whose names are affixed to its parts, because we have lost the autograph copies and the text has been edited out of manuscripts of a later day; for part of your education consists in teaching you the facts concerning the transmission of ancient books, and you are reading to-day, without a shadow of doubt as to their genuineness, the love-poems of Catullus to Lesbia, when we know that our existing text was made out of a single manuscript that turned up in Verona in the fourteenth century. Differences of opinion among theologians and the rancor of theological debate will appear as shallow arguments with you—though they are sometimes urged as possessing great importance—against the possibility of any knowledge upon the topics they concern; for there is hardly a subject in your curriculum that has not had a history of conflicting sentiments and that is not at this moment represented by rival schools.

I regard the conditions of your training here as favorable in the highest degree to your religious life. You are receiving a discipline of your powers that should save you from the sophistries to which the uneducated fall such easy victims. You are acquiring a knowledge of the great subjects of debate, and an estimate of the men who have most right to be regarded as authorities respecting them, that will keep you from calling any man master whose only claim to such recognition is his entertaining declamation. Besides that, you are dealing with secular themes under Christian conceptions, and your attention is turned to the specific evidences that accredit those Christian conceptions. There is also an undergraduate sentiment represented by the ripest scholars and the men of highest intellectual rank among us that is not only favorable to Christian life, but also aggressively and earnestly interested in Christian work. So that, if your religious life is not strengthened and stimulated by your connection with the college, the fault will not be with the college, but with you.

I know that there is a band of Christian young men in this college who are self-denying and unsparing of effort and pains in their endeavor to bring religious motives to bear upon their fellow-students; and I can hope for nothing better for some of you than that you may come within the scope of their influence. I speak with due allowance for temptations that beset students in every college, but I am nevertheless of the opinion that there are no circumstances under which a man is so likely to receive good impressions, and to be affected by religious influences that will abide through his whole life, as during the four years of a college course in an institution founded, as this is, upon Christian principles, and administered with special regard to the maintenance of vital piety. But I must remind you of the personal responsibility that you should feel in this matter. You can make your college career very much what you choose to make it. I hope that it will prove a blessing to you, and that you will go out into the world with a larger equipment of both faith and knowledge. But to secure this result a great deal depends upon yourselves, and what you will do will be determined very largely by the way you begin. Better late than never, is a good motto; but—better not be late. It is better to begin right than to discover toward the close of the year that you have made a mistake.

Let me counsel you, then, to make your life in college a religious life; to interest yourselves in religious matters; to identify yourselves with the Christian elements in the college that seek your coöperation; and to give studious regard to the maintenance of religious habits and the fostering of religious convictions.

Let your religion control your college life, and then you may rest assured that your college life will react in strengthening, maturing, deepening, broadening, and elevating your Christian faith.

THE LETTER AND THE SPIRIT.*

BY PRESIDENT FRANCIS L. PATTON, D.D., LL.D.

"For the letter killeth, but the spirit giveth life."—2 COR. 3:6.

THERE is no doubt, I suppose, that when the Apostle made use of this familiar antithesis he intended in the first place to distinguish between the Law and the Gospel; between the written code, with its rigid requirements, which can only awaken a sense of helplessness and only intensify the feeling of loss, and the indwelling, grace-bestowing, comfort-giving Spirit. But it can hardly be questioned that the words of this verse may be properly used in a wider sense, and that this wider sense is at least implicitly recognized by the Apostle himself. I should only be illustrating the truth of the text understood in this broader sense were I to insist upon a literalism of interpretation that would tolerate no application of it outside of the sphere within which it was originally employed; and I think I can better serve the purpose I have in view to-day, and can better adapt

---
* A baccalaureate sermon.

my discourse to the circumstances of this time and place, by taking advantage of some of the more obvious contrasts which these words are so well fitted to suggest.

I. It is true that the word *pneuma* here has special reference to the Holy Spirit, but it also signifies the human spirit, and, with the word *gramma* as the other term of the antithesis, I think there is nothing violent or strained in making the suggested contrast between Language and Thought the first topic for consideration.

Thought and not the mode of its expression, mind and not the drapery in which it is enveloped, should be our first concern. It is fatal to elevating work to let energy terminate in the letter. The aim of the true scholar is to go behind the letter to the spirit. The bare suggestion of language as the means of communicating thought presents to us one of the most wonderful facts in life. It is the commonplace, after all, that is the most mysterious. Thought leaps the chasm of two separate personalities and excites no wonder. We lay bare the secrets of our inner life to each other and then wonder at *actio in distans* and cavil at the possibility of divine communication. So easy is it to strain at the gnat and swallow the camel.

To think and speak; to have ideas and register

them; to make ourselves plain; to find a common measure of thought among the many coins of speech; to converse with our contemporaries in the morning newspaper and hold fellowship with the dead in the books that keep their memories alive—this, if we only stopped to consider it, is the marvel of existence. A mystery, I grant, and one made no easier of solution by the suicidal philosopher who tries through pages of labored excogitation to reduce thought to mechanism, and then sends his book with his compliments to the courteous reader, in the hope that he will think that the author is a thinker of uncommon intellect in thus demonstrating with such convincing logic, and such array of physiological testimony, that there is no thought and no thinker at all.

Thought is mind's protest against materialism. We need no other. Language is thought's portrait, the print of thought's finger. It is easy to see, therefore, why the study of language, as distinguished from literature, should occupy a high place in the academic curriculum. It is of great moment to understand the forms of thought, to follow its curves and watch its subtleties and niceties of distinction, as we are able to do after it has been hardened and colored in speech. You may learn a great deal of psychology from the Greek prepositions. The subjunctive mood will often prove a shorter road to the human mind than the psychometric experiments of Fechner and Wundt. We may, however, make too much of philology; and even though we had to be satisfied with less grammar, I would have more literature. Let us read Milton rather than read about him, and read him as we love to read him rather than at the snail's pace indicated by Ruskin. Give us the story of Achilles in the pages of Derby and Bryant if we must choose between an English translation and a few dog's-eared pages of the Greek original.

Βῆ δ' ἀκέων παρὰ θῖνα πολυφλοίσβοιο θαλάσσης—

the line is a picture; the rhythm is exquisite; the sound an echo of the sense. Give us time to follow Chryses as he moves sadly along the shore, and let this vision of beauty excuse us from the "principal parts" of βαίνω; for the letter killeth, but the spirit giveth life. Translation is difficult work, as we have been so recently reminded by Mr. Pater and Mr. Lowell. To do it well requires that we should know the letter, but it requires also—what is more difficult to attain—that we should catch the spirit of the author, that we should see with his eyes and rethink his thoughts. It is a pretty conceit of Marion Crawford which leads him, in one of his later works, to represent his hero as taking advantage of the recent advances in electrical science —thereby removing the barriers that separate him from the unseen world—and holding face-to-face fellowship "with the immortals." This is exactly what a liberal education is intended to do. This is what it has done for you, if you have improved your opportunities here, unless our methods are deplorably bad. This is why we learn Latin and Greek and master the difficulties of vocabulary. I do not deny that it is of advantage to know the laws of phonetic change, and that there is intellectual training in the knowledge of word forms. But when classical training is useful only as dumb-bells and parallel-bars are useful, it is writing a commentary on my text. Master syntax for disciplinary ends; and master it also, as Richard de Bury says, that we may thereby open royal roads into literature. But remember that the thought is more than the word; that at best the word is but a symbol, a suggestion of the thought, and rarely its equivalent. He who reads literally reads poorly. Even jurisprudence, the science that holds speech to strictest account, admits that there are times when we must not only judge what a man intends to say by what he says, but what he says by what he obviously meant to say. *Hæret in literâ, hæret in cortice.*

There is too little classical study of the purely literary kind among us. We either know as specialists and know little else, or we know practically nothing. And it is probably hard to unite the functions of the general and the special scholar. Few men can expend energy on the letter sufficient to write the notes to Mayor's "Juvenal," and then write an "advertisement" to the volume that quivers in every line with sympathetic interest in the questions of the day.

I say nothing regarding letters which is not true of science also. For the facts which the man of science handles are only the letters with which he is trying to spell out the thought embodied in them. He may amuse himself with the shapes of these letters, put them in bundles and give them names, but so long as he is simply engaged with facts he is employed in business no better than playing chess or solving puzzles. It is when he hits upon some key to Nature's cipher, it is when he is using his facts in verification of an hypothesis that stands for thought, that he is doing work worthy of scientific fame. Otherwise he is only a census-taker in the kingdom of nature; a cataloguer in the library of truth, writing titles and reading the backs of books.

Let not the humanist, however, speak to the disparagement of science, for if he is only using language as material for the exercise of his own thought, if the results of his labors are not the basis of generalizations that stand for thought, then he is simply collecting facts, gathering useless knowledge, printing interminable masses of unreadable material. And indeed this, to a large extent, is the condition of things to-day. We are over-specializing; and the danger is that our scholars will become simply operatives under a great system of contract labor; full of opinions on subjects of which we have no knowledge, and full of knowledge on subjects that give no basis for opinion. We are overwhelmed with material, and in danger of being submerged in the mass of facts which we cannot reduce to system. How often, as we see ambition spurred to new endeavor, are we reminded of these words of the text: the letter killeth, the spirit giveth life.

Ah, Science, you want fact! You proclaim the sovereignty of fact, the reign of law, the almightiness of induction, the empire of sense. Your votaries have reduced history to science, and philosophy to science, and religion to science, and language to science; and when you have done all, what have you gained? A mass of unorganized material; a box of Chinese puzzles; a rubbish-heap of monographs on Greek adverbs, Coptic manuscripts, Babylonian pottery, the Pythagorean theory of the universe, and so forth, without order and without plan—or else there is a thought, an idea, a generalization behind it all. The destiny of it all is death and the dunghill, or else there is some informing, quickening idea to give it shape and comeliness. Do your best: the philosopher, the apostle of the idea, is needed to make these dry bones live.

Whose thought, then, lies behind this language of fact? Is it your subjective state that you have been imposing upon Nature as the law of her operations when you have formulated the doctrine of gravitation? Is it your subjectivity that imposes a meaning upon "Hamlet" and "Faust," no thanks to Shakespeare and Goethe? Will you split the difference between the two rival philosophers by an arbitrary decision to be objective in your recognition of the fact, and subjective in your explanation of the fact? Or will you see behind the letter the spirit; behind the fact the idea that gives meaning to the fact and makes you a sharer in the thought of God? I do not wonder that the man of science magnifies his office and feels proud of his high calling. Back of the barriers of speech, indeed, that melt away with our knowledge of a foreign tongue, stand "the immortals," and we may converse with them to our heart's content. But back of the syllables of science, and waiting only for the spirit of reverence for its enjoyment, lies fellowship with God.

The literary artist has recalcitrant material to deal with. With the author thought is too volatile, and with the translator language is too opaque. So that between the incapacity of the containing vessel and the chance of spilling in our attempts to decant it into another, we run the risk of losing some of the wine of genius. This is true of human thought; how much more true must it be of divine thought. We cannot give too much attention, then, to the very words in which our Bible is written, and the more fully we believe in its inspiration, the more anxious we shall be to have a correct text and a close translation. But we may have both and miss the spirit of revelation. We may have a bald literalism of rendering that sacrifices good English to Greek idiom, and saves the letter at the expense of the spirit. We may load our memory with "various readings," and be so microscopic in our study of the text as to be unable to see the full contour of a divine idea. We may carry reverence for the Word to the extent of being undiscriminating worshipers of words, and by our unintelligent literalism miss the meaning that the words convey. When I find men treating metaphor as fact and reading poetry as they would construe an act of Congress, seeking a spiritual sense in every commonplace expression, missing the point of the parable of the prodigal son by asking who was the " elder brother," and invoking the joint assistance of chemistry and the Book of Leviticus in the interpretation of the parable of the leaven, I feel that Matthew Arnold, with all his faults, at least deserves credit for reminding us that the Bible is to be treated as literature. But we must go further before we can be said to have passed beyond the letter in our study of Scripture. For though as literature it may be read with due regard to the historical conditions under which it was produced, with proper attention to differences of style and form of composition, we have not read it as we should when we have mastered its geographical details, studied its archæology, learned to prize the beauties of Isaiah and Job, or appreciate the high moral level of the Sermon on the Mount. To regard the Bible simply as literature provokes in me a feeling akin to that which I have for the system once in vogue of making the Gospel of John an easy introduction to the study of Greek. We degrade the book by teaching it under false pretenses. We dishonor truth when we teach it with a *suppressio veri*. I am in full sympathy with the idea that the Bible—the English

Bible, if you like that way of describing it better—should have a place in the college curriculum; but I want it understood that it is to be taught with distinct regard to its divine authority and the great doctrines of redemption that it contains.

You have made but a poor use of your facilities here, my friends, if you are not able to make the distinction I have named. This indeed is no small part of education. We have tried to train you so as to bring you under the power of ideas. We have aimed to educate you so that you may become scholars, and not pedants; jurists, and not pettifoggers; men of science, and not the bottle-washers of a laboratory; theologians, and not textualists; religious men who think again through God's Word the thoughts of God, and not dealers in cant phrases or slaves of a stupid literalism.

II. The same antithesis with which we are dealing may serve also to stand for the contrast between the accidental and the essential in matters of literary judgment and of religious opinions. Print does not discriminate. Even punctuation is a modern device, and jurisprudence disdains it to this day. It gives no weight to the commas and semicolons with which we sprinkle our pages, sometimes in default of a clear style or a correct syntax. It allows no vulgar italics to lend artificial emphasis to what is written, but leaves the thought to make its way to the mind with no other presupposition than the intelligence of the reader. This is indeed often a large demand, but there seems to be as yet no sufficient substitute for brains; and to one normally furnished in this regard it is a self-evident proposition that, though the printed word does not say so, all thoughts are not of equal value nor worthy of the same emphasis. No obligation rests upon us, for instance, to treat all the poet's verse as of equal beauty and force because he has not seen fit to show any favoritism to the children of his brain. It is not our fault that there are only three lines worth remembering in Wordsworth's "Peter Bell." All that is said is not worth repeating. All human deeds are not worth recording. Worthless when new, they do not gain importance with the lapse of time. The phonograph that listens to-day and reproduces the nonsense of conversation a hundred years hence will amuse, but it will not edify. It occurs to me to say this when I consider the prevalent mania for original research. Just now it is affecting historians and men of letters. You may know history—you may have your Gibbon, your Hallam, and your Freeman at your fingers' ends—but you are no historian unless you have studied the sources. If, however, you have discovered a manuscript that will add a new chapter to the life of some tenth-rate Cavalier or Roundhead, if you can come forth from your labors with the dust of an old library on your fingers, you have earned the title to fame. But why? Why discriminate thus against the man who knows much in favor of him who produces little? Do I deny that your work is good? By no means. That you have brought something new to light, and so have made a contribution to knowledge? No. Or that your work has given you good training in the use of tools? No. Nor would I deny that it is a useful thing for our young civil engineers to survey the college campus every year, or measure the Brooklyn Bridge. I am only thinking that you lack perspective; that you are mistaking pains and trouble and a monopoly of useless information for history; that you are in danger of putting all facts upon the same level and of ranking the genealogy of a Mayflower family with the Norman Conquest. You are deceived by the letter and miss the spirit. You have adopted Gradgrind's philosophy. The demand is for facts, and so it comes to pass that in the examination paper Oklahoma counts for as much as Thermopylæ, and the date of the last constitutional amendment is thought to have as good a right to a vacant memory cell as A.D. 1453 or 1688.

We read books and study the history of opinion often with the same disregard of proportion—remembering what we ought to forget and forgetting what we ought to remember; making no allowance for circumstances, and giving the same value to *obiter dicta* that we accord to reasoned opinions. Find Calvin tripping in a casual remark, then vilify his system: this is what men do. Or because one calls himself a disciple of Augustine, hold him responsible for all that Augustine taught, as though one must believe in the virtues of tar-water because he is a Berkleyan.

Uneducated men, perhaps, find it hard to make the distinctions between essence and accident here referred to. All statements appear to them like items on a ledger to be reckoned in the same way. But educated men ought to know better. They ought to know that a man can be a Lutheran without believing all that Luther believed, or accept the Hegelian conception of the universe without sympathizing in detail with Hegel's peculiar views. It ought not to be difficult to understand that a creed statement may be accurate in doctrinal content though colored by the time in which it was written, and dealing with conditions of thought that no longer exist. And it must also be evident that it would be hard to avoid the appearance of anachronism if we undertook to weave the thoughts of this generation into a document that on its title-page purports to have been written two hundred and fifty years ago. A little exercise of judgment, however, a little effort to distinguish between essence and accident, abiding fact and accidental setting—in short, to read the spirit in the letter would save all the trouble.

We may as well learn to exercise this power of judgment on the creeds, for we shall have to exercise it on the Scriptures. All Scripture is inspired, but it does not all possess the same religious value. All Scripture is truth, but all Scriptural truth is not of equal importance. Essential to the organic structure of the Bible all of it undoubtedly is, but not equally essential to spiritual life and religious education. When men say they wish the Bible to be taught without doctrine, I reply that the doctrines of the Bible are more important than much of the Bible itself. The sense of Scripture is the Scripture, and rather than miss the sense we could afford to do without certain forms of Bible knowledge. There is in the Bible, as in other literature, what may be called the essential and the accidental, and it is an act of intelligence to distinguish between them. I read the Cosmogony and get out of it the doctrine of creation, the ascent of life, the supremacy of man and his primeval purity. I am willing to fill up the great categories of Genesis with the help of science, and so make the generalizations that follow the study of one of God's books help in the interpretation of the other. I read in the words of the Saviour the generic ideas that should control social existence and the great principles that should guide conduct, but I do not suppose that the illustration of a principle should be construed with literal exactness. I do not expect to handle venomous reptiles with impunity. I do not expect faith to supersede medical treatment or cure organic disease; and I do not find either in the Sermon on the Mount or in the apostolic community of goods an argument for socialism and the denial of the rights of property. I believe that Paul was inculcating an important principle when he discouraged the appearance of Christians as litigants in heathen courts; but I would not on that account conclude that all litigation is sin, and that the legal profession is incompatible with Christianity. To be sure the distinction between essence and accident involves serious responsibility, for in attempting to make it we may err. I am sure that Arnold erred and that his literary judgment was warped by his prejudices when he made ethics the main thing in Scripture and represented the dogmas of Christianity as the accidents of Pauline teaching. For what is the Bible? What is the evolution of Biblical ideas but the growth of a few great dogmatic conceptions? The essence of Scripture, the core of the Old Testament and the New, is the doctrine that without the shedding of blood there is no remission of sins, and that God was in Christ reconciling the world unto himself, not imputing unto men their trespasses. It is the divine purpose that brings the Bible into line with the facts of the material world. It is the Incarnation that gives organic character to Scripture. It is human guilt that constitutes the great presupposition of Revelation. It is the doctrine of faith as man's response to the overtures of love that meets the exigencies of man's moral nature and makes the Bible the best and greatest message that man ever had. Why, then, do men tell me that they wish the Bible taught religiously but not doctrinally? Why do educated men who have been taught to distinguish between the letter and the spirit show such proneness to mistake when they touch religious themes? Yet the world is full of men who speak in this way. These are the men who stand in our pulpits and preach on the patience of Job and the moral courage of Daniel; who find material for sentimental sermons in the seasons, and entertaining sermons in the social follies of the day, and practical sermons in the importance of sleep or the need of restricting immigration, but who are silent respecting the tremendous fact of sin and the dogmatic significance of atoning blood. I do not say that such men are handling the Word of God deceitfully, for I am willing to have them plead guilty, if they prefer, to an unscholarly stupidity that prevents them from seeing that the bleeding Christ is the central fact of Scripture.

Let me beg you, gentlemen, to heed this lesson of the text. Cultivate a wise discrimination. Read the best books. Seize upon master thoughts. Get hold of the big end of the questions that invite your scrutiny. Distinguish between what is vital and what is of no importance. Garner the wheat; let the chaff go. Rest your opinions on broad and deep rational foundations. Follow this method in religion. A few principles, a few facts, carry the whole fabric of Christianity. Follow the great trend of evidence, and do not halt for minor difficulties. Let the great outlying facts of Christianity determine your faith, and do not let trifles feed your doubt. You are sticking in the bark, you may be sure, when you let a textual difficulty, or an historical discrepancy, or a hard question in ethics, or a dogmatic mystery, hinder your acceptance of the historic Christ as the Saviour of the world.

III. I come now to the consideration of another distinction suggested by the text. It is difficult to resist the feeling that there was in Paul's mind the contrast between the rigid fixity of the letter on the one hand and the plastic spontaneity of the spirit on the other. *Litera scripta manet.* The written word does not change. But the living organism is constantly adjusting itself to new conditions, and changing to suit them. We have then the fixed and the variable, unbending law and changing life. The history of the world, of society, of religious opinion, is to a large extent the history of these two factors in their relations to each other. The legal code becomes too narrow to suit the exigencies of an expanding life, and it changes in fact but not in form. The needed work is done, but the forms of law are saved by legal fiction. *Ubi jus ibi remedium;* but there is no remedy at common law, and equity finds one through the edict of the prætor or the decisions of the chancellor. We have a written constitution as the basis of government, and the powers of the coördinate branches of government are defined. But time develops the old conflict between the unyielding law and the living organism, with the odds, as Professor Wilson shows, in favor of the organism. We formulate our faith in creed statements, and after a century or two find that the Church and the creed are not in exact accord. There is nothing to wonder at. It is the old question of the letter and the spirit. The letter has controlled the life. It has given the law to its variations. Political development in this land will follow the lines of the Constitution. Theological development will follow the lines of the creed that controls it. Unless the letter·goes into the life of the organism it will become a dead letter; and if it goes into it, it will be modified and colored by circumstances of time and place.

Now this question of the fixed and the variable is a much larger one than that of creed revision. It is at the root of nearly all the great questions of to-day. Men are realizing as never before the solidarity of mankind. The old Pelagian conception of individualism is abandoned and there is a tendency to go to the opposite extreme. Individual opinion is hushed in the presence of advancing waves and irresistible movements, as they are called, and we are warned against the folly of trying to stop the rising tide. In the case of very advanced thinkers this worship of the *Zeitgeist* is associated with the denial of all *a priori* ideas. Standards of measurement there are none. The movement is recognized, but there is no criterion by which to judge it, and the ideas that limit it and give it shape are ignored. Men say we must study the facts in an historical spirit and gather our induction out of what we see. The science of ethics becomes the science of what is, rather than of what ought to be, and if a doctrine of right survives at all, it is the doctrine that whatever is is right.

In the name of reason I protest against this tendency of thought. As a sovereign thinker within the realm of my own activities, I refuse to abdicate under the terrorism of popular sentiment. I refuse to say that because the avalanche is irresistible, therefore it is right. I refuse to drown my reason in a tidal wave. And when any idea in philosophy or politics or theology is "in the air," I claim the right to examine its credentials and scrutinize its claims before I give it my acceptance. Historic movements, as well as the actions of individual men, must be judged by fixed principles. It is easy, then, for me to define my position in regard to what is called progressive theology. Will you tie the Church to the letter or give her the free life of the spirit? How will you adjust the relations between the letter and the spirit; the Church and the creed; the organism and the law of its development? According to Schleiermacher, the New Testament is only the recorded religious experience of the apostolic age, genetically related to the ages following, but giving no rubric and imposing no law. It follows, then, that there is no standard of faith, that truth is relative, and that the Christian organism is a law unto itself. The Roman Catholic, again, says that the organism is infallible and can speak in the present tense. It is not necessary, therefore, to believe that all divine revelation is contained in the Bible. Transubstantiation came by way of doctrinal evolution with the second council of Nice, and papal infallibility within the present generation. The doctrine of evolution applied to theology by Cardinal Newman helps Rome to adjust the relation between the fixed and the variable. Protestants, however, have the written word as their only rule of faith. Changing taste cannot obliterate its doctrines. Organic drifts cannot vacate words of their historic sense. We cannot eliminate doctrines because we do not like them, or insert new ones because popular sentiment calls for them. What is written is written. The Christian consciousness can no more change the meaning of a Greek word than it can upset the multiplication table. There is no legal fiction that can modify or change the Word of God. When men say, as in effect they do, that the old conception of a sovereign God does not suit our republican ideas, they only blaspheme. And when by-and-by they will seek to dethrone him and plainly say that each generation must elect its own Ruler and dictate his administrative policy, they will only carry to their logical consequences some of the prevalent ideas of to-day.

I do not deny, however, that important truth is hinted at in the doctrine known as the Christian Consciousness. I am no advocate of ecclesiastical immobility. The Christian Church is not an exact copy in mode of worship, methods of administration, and form of government of the Church of the New Testament. We have discontinued the holy kiss, and feet washing is no part of Christian hospitality. We have salaried ministers and surpliced choirs, neither being known to the Apostolic Church. We have tried to foster the apostolic spirit and perpetuate apostolic ideas, but the Church has altered her mode of life and work to suit altered conditions of society. Paul said that under certain circumstances he would refuse the meat offered in sacrifice to idols, and would not drink wine that had any idolatrous associations. Interpret him literally and his words have no application to modern life, for the conditions that controlled his decision no longer exist. Change his decision into a mandate of abstinence and at once you tyrannize over the conscience and rob the act of abstinence of all ethical significance. Generalize the statement, however, and you have the great law of altruistic morality which, after all abatements for selfishness have been made, is the most potent factor in our practical life.

And so with doctrine. The dogmas of Christianity are fixed. The Bible does not change and we have no extra-biblical revelation. But a dogma that is only read in the Bible or stated and subscribed to in a creed is only a dead letter. It must go into our life and be part of our intellectual and moral experience. But going into our individual and our organic life it adjusts itself to changing conditions, although unchanged itself. It will be read with a different emphasis in different periods; it will be interpreted in the light of the burning questions of those periods; it will be brought into relation with science and philosophy, and acquire fresh interest from generation to generation from the new polemic conditions that are constantly emerging. Paul's vocabulary was affected by his contact with philosophy. Ours will be. The attempt to eliminate philosophy from theology is a vain attempt. The two departments deal largely with the same subjects and cover common ground. All the material, whatever be its source, whatever be its authority, that goes to make our theory of the universe must pass into our life and bear the impress of our thought; and as we think in philosophy so we shall be compelled to think in theology. We handle the same questions regarding God, freedom, and immortality that Paul did, that Augustine did, that Thomas Aquinas did, that Calvin did; and though the Scriptures have not changed, and our reading of them, so far as these topics are concerned, is not materially different from that of the men that have been named, we see the same truth under different conditions. Our heretics are not Cerinthus and Celsus, but Spencer and Kuenen. Our foe is not credulity, but agnosticism. And as conditions change, our mode of presenting the unchangeable truth must also change. Remember, however, that if the letter without the life is dead, the life needs the letter to give law to its movement. Do not be deceived by the cry that the voice of the people is the voice of God. Do not hastily assume that every great movement is an inspired movement. We have no personal infallibility. We believe in no corporate infallibility. We have no faith in the inspiration of large masses of men. When, therefore, under the influence of those who would have us put our faith in the organism rather than tie it to the written word, we begin to lose faith in the authority of Scripture, we give up our only basis of Christian certitude.

IV. The letter killeth, the spirit giveth life. Outward rule and inward principle are the two great agencies that operate on human conduct, and they seem contrasted in the text. There is the inner principle in bent of inclination and dominant purpose seeking expression in our spontaneities; and here is the objective code by which we seek to guide our life, and which is put before us as an instructive and restraining influence. The world, says Mr. Lecky, is governed by its ideals. It is what we love to do that we do well. By help of rule alone men write no books and paint no pictures that wear the stamp of genius. They perform no acts of heroism in grudging compliance with law; they shine in none of the beauties of high and holy character when they have simply schooled themselves to follow another's will. Work done in conformity with rule is drudgery and a weariness of the flesh. There is the morality of principle and the morality of outward conformity. That there is a place for the morality of externalism and precept, of law and obedience to command, I do not doubt, yet I sometimes think that life is made more burdensome than it need be, and that we hinder rather than help the higher interests of morality by the excessive multiplication of rules. The State goes as far as it ought in encroaching upon the freedom of the individual; the Church is taking liberties with the rights of conscience in saying that its members shall do this and shall not do that. We go to college and a code of instructions is the first lesson we are required to learn. We enter business and we find ourselves girt about by rule. We are more unwilling every day to assume that men will act right from principle, and more disposed to think that they love to do wrong. Wholesale suspicion is the law of society. We are multiplying the machinery of detection. We cry, Who will keep the keepers? We are insuring ourselves at increasing cost against the dishonesty of those whom we have trusted. We watch the clerk at his desk and the student in his examination. We put a bell-punch in the hands of the conductor and set traps for the night watchman. In forms more or less visible and in ways more or less irritating to the feelings, we proclaim our inability to trust men and our conviction that all men are liars.

Necessary all this may be for protection, though I still believe that we owe more to conscience than to all our complicated machinery of police. But the trouble is that men suppose that all this is moral education. There is an impression that you make men moral when you make them fear to do wrong, and that by repressing wrong-doing you are elevating character. Make wrong-doing so difficult that right-doing will be easier and it is thought you will make men moral. And undoubtedly a great deal of the world's morality is of this sort. A man obeys the law because he fears the penalty. He will lose his place, or incur the odium of society, or be visited with social ostracism, or miss his diploma, and therefore he will do as he is told. And there are good men who fail to see that there is no morality in this. Not only do they fail to see it, but the opinion seems to be gaining ground that we can build up character by this system of externalisms. Men not only obey laws imposed by society for its own protection, but they take pledges, make promises, multiply vows for their own edification, and in place of the freedom of the spirit they are going back to the legalism of an older dispensation, are rejoicing in the bondage of the letter.

They should know, however, that enforced obedience is not moral education. Character is an endogenous plant and grows from within. Military training teaches men to obey law, but it does not teach them to love it. Deserters are shot; so the soldier does not desert. That is all. Kant is right. The law that comes from without is not ethical. There is no morality in doing right through calculation of consequences. Hence only self-legislated law is moral. Though it be God's law, it must be autonomous before it is ethical. It must address the conscience and be approved as good. It must become a maxim of reason and not a mere command. For the letter killeth, but the Spirit giveth life. The State, of course, must protect itself, and its main end is therefore not moral education. This must be left to the Church. But what is to be our aim in the administration of a college? Shall we consider the good order of the organization, or the moral improvement of the student? It might be easy to do either; it may be hard to combine the two; but we must combine them. There must be rules, but they should be few, and the application of them should address the conscience. We must prepare men for the franchises which they are so soon to inherit, by respecting their manhood and avoiding all petty legislation. We must protect the organism and at the same time labor for the good of the individual. We must hold law subservient to the end for which it is enacted and bend the rule if it be necessary in order to save the man. We must consider, it is true, the welfare of the mass, but we must sometimes, if need be, leave the ninety-and-nine, and care for the one who has gone astray.

The college student is ingenuous, as a rule. He makes mistakes and falls into mischief or sin. But the case is rare when you do not find something in him that draws you to him. He is frank. He will admit that he has abused kindness, trifled with good-nature, and acted meanly. He is sorry that he did so, and his climax of regret is generally the thought of his mother's anguish and his father's sorrow. I have a large place in my heart for the man who is capable of this filial love. But, my brother, you must stand on higher ground than this. You are going out to face the temptations of the world. You will be confronted with the lust of the flesh, the lust of the eye, and the pride of life. It is not enough that you recognize the authority of the outward law. You should make it an inner principle. It is not enough that wrong conduct be avoided because it is dishonorable and will bring disgrace. Learn to avoid it because it is wrong. Learn to do right because it is right.

Learn to feel the sanctions of a higher morality, and when your evil-doing fills you with regret let it be because you have sinned against God and put a stain upon your soul.

V. And now, gentlemen of the graduating class, let me say a single closing word. This week marks an important era in the calendar of your life. It means the severance of old ties; the full assumption of personal responsibility, and the facing of the future. We have tried hard to fit you for the work of life. We have not done what we might have done; partly perhaps through our neglect, partly also through your neglect. But to some extent in all of you, I trust, and to a large extent in most of you, I know, our aim has been realized. In sending you out into the world we are making a contribution to its working force of which we have no reason to be ashamed. We have tried to make the education we have given you a commentary upon the words that I have chosen for my text. We have tried to foster in you high ideals in literature and high aims in science. We have tried to discipline your powers so that you will see the parts of truth in their proper relations to each other and in just proportion. We have tried to show that the unchanging Word of God is not a fossil to be laid upon the shelf, but the directing principle of the life, the inspiration of its movement, and the law of its variation. We have tried to teach you also that the essence of all morality is a self-enunciated law of obligation, commanding without condition and despising calculation.

And we have not forgotten in the services of this sanctuary that the contrast between the letter and the spirit bears witness also to another contrast between Law and Gospel, to which reference was made in the beginning of this discourse. The Apostle did not mean to disparage the Law when he contrasted it with the Gospel. The Gospel did not supersede the Law, it only supplemented it. The Law is holy, just, and good. It came from God, and is the expression of his will. It is perfect but unrelenting. It tells us what we ought to do. It sets before us an ideal that excites our admiration and provokes despair. You accept it as just, but you cannot comply with it. You resolve and fail. You promise and break your vow. You make an effort and fall short. But the Law accepts no excuse and makes no allowance. There is no pity in its tones. It meets your contrition with no encouraging word. Its face is rigid and its voice is hard. Your passing grade, it tells you, is a hundred, and you have failed. That is all it has to say. It measures; it does not pity. It tabulates results; it does not forgive.

The Law is the embodiment of God's will, but there is also another embodiment of that will. And when, conscious of your failure, you go to Jesus and say, "O Master, I know I ought to have done better, and I feel ashamed," then will come a look of such exquisite tenderness upon his face that will say before the words are spoken, Thy sins are forgiven thee; go in peace. When, after fruitless endeavor to learn the lessons of life and do its work, we go to him and say, "O Divine Teacher, I would fain learn, but I am very slow, and my poor powers are not equal to this high task," he will say to you again, "Have patience, child, and I will teach thee. I will put my Spirit within thee. I will perfect my strength in thy weakness." The Law came by Moses, but grace and truth came by Jesus Christ. Have fellowship with Christ. Walk with him. Turn ever to him for comfort, for strength, for guidance. Serve him while you live, and by-and-by you shall be like him, and you shall see him as he is.

CHRIST AS A MAN OF PRAYER.

BY PROF. JAMES O. MURRAY, D.D., LL.D.

"And it came to pass in those days, that he went out into a mountain to pray, and continued all night in prayer to God."
—LUKE 6:12.

ALMOST every thoughtful person has known moods in which the solitude and silence of nature came like balm upon the hurt soul. It was refreshing and comforting to get away from contact with man, from vices that disgust us, and pettiness that vexes us, and deceit that affronts us, into contact with the calm, sweet refreshings of nature and communion with God. So we may suppose our Lord, only in an immeasurably purer spirit, to have betaken himself gladly from the unbelief and the hardness, from the mercenary spirit of the loaves and fishes and the hateful Pharisaic pride, from the misery and the degradation, into this mountain-top far from all sights or sounds of man. "The scene of this lonely vigil is the same, in all probability, as that of the Sermon on the Mount." As described by recent observers, "it is a hill with a summit which closely resembles an Oriental saddle with its two high peaks. On the west it rises very little above the level of a broad and undulating plain; on the east it sinks precipitately toward a plateau, on which lies, immediately beneath the cliffs, the village of Hattin; and from this plateau the traveler descends through a wild and tropic gorge to the shining levels of the Lake of Galilee. It is the only conspicuous hill on the western side of the lake, and it is singularly adapted by its conformation both to form a place for short retirement and a rendezvous for gathering multitudes." Hither at nightfall, alone, weary, burdened with a world's redemption, came Christ to pray. The stars came out one by one above him, the silence deepened around him as the night wore on, and when, after midnight had passed and the morning star stood in the heavens, the first ray of dawn tipped the trans-Jordanic hills, Christ was still in this communion with his Father. It is not, then, so much Christ fleeing from the harassing, disappointing, mournful contact with men and men's sins and miseries into the vernal quiet and refreshing beauty of nature, as it is Christ in this night of prayer on a mountain-top disclosing to man prayer in the highest ranges of spiritual experience, which arrests us and challenges an eager and a solemn attention. *Christ's devotional habits or Christ as a man of prayer* gives us our theme.

In the outset, and before any attempt is made to combine in one picture the scattered notices of his prayers, it should be noted that there is something wonderfully attractive and powerfully suggestive in this view of Christ. It contrasts so mightily with that of the same Christ stilling tempests, casting out evil spirits, raising the dead. And this not only as it reverses Christ's position, bringing him to his knees or on his face as a supplicant for help, whereas winds and seas and devils and the very dead had but just obeyed his voice, but still more as it shows him entered into our deepest and most sacred human experiences, those of communion with God in prayer, in sore soul-struggles, in solitary, anxious, possibly bitter experiences. To gain any fit impression of how deeply and pervasively prayer entered into the human life of Christ, we must study the four Gospels and put together their separate notices of his devotional life. Over the life of Jesus preparatory to his public ministry, that thirty years at Nazareth, for the most part a thick veil hangs. But this we *do* know, that he was trained in the Old Testament Scriptures, and the spirit of the Old Testament Scriptures is the spirit of prayer all the way through, from Jacob's wrestling with the Angel to Daniel's supplications toward Jerusalem. How natural, then, to find, as we do find, that his public ministry began, as it ended, in prayer. "Now when all the people were baptized, it came to pass, that Jesus also being baptized, and *praying*, the heaven was opened." That opened heaven was the avenue through which his supplications found their way to God his Father till death closed his lips in silence. The Evangelists are not effusive and declamatory on this theme. They even treat it with a sacred reserve, seldom lifting the veil from the sacred privacy. But whenever it *is* lifted, what we see rivets the impression that prayerfulness comes into the life of Jesus in no secondary nor incidental way, but as its undertone, its substrata on which his public life and ministry repose. The Evangelists have singled out instances of Christ's devotions, his prayers at the remarkable junctures of his history—when he was baptized, when he was transfigured, when he chose the twelve apostles, when one of them was to be sifted like wheat, when he was to be separated from his disciples, when his soul was coming under its great agony, and when he bowed his head to death. The impression which such records make on us is that these prayers are the indexes to his whole life as a life of prayerfulness. They suggest to us the fact that he made so much of prayer as to avail himself of every possible outward aid to devotion. He who was careful to instruct men that they were to enter into their closet and shut to the door and pray to God in secret—he sought the stillness of night-seasons and mountain-tops, the calming influences of perfect solitude far from the madding crowd. These notices disclose to us the fact that Christ's devotional life here and there came out in transcendent intensity and volume, taking for its needed expression whole nights upon mountain-tops. Pause a moment and think of Christ's praying through that night, from watch to watch, till the breaking day called him to labor. We know not for what he prayed, we know not what blessedness of heavenly communion or what agonies of wrestling supplication the still heavens above him witnessed; whether Gethsemane were foreshadowed or Hermon renewed. If, however, we notice carefully the fact that in all such records prayer holds a prominent place in what may be called the *emergencies* of Christ's history, we cannot fail to be impressed by such prayers as revelations of Christ's devotional life. For being made in all things like unto his brethren, there came to him, as there come to all of us, critical periods in life, when existence suddenly takes on deeper responsibilities. It is some grave question to affect the whole future of life for us—a change which will surely project its influences into eternity for ourselves and for those dear to us. It is the memorable thing in the history of the Redeemer that he entered on no such period without prayer. Look again at that night of prayer on the mountain-top. Consider to what it is the prelude. The time has come for the Saviour to associate with himself the men who were to be the founders of his Church on earth. The whole future of that Church is to be affected by the transaction. It is the question of Peter and James and John. His selection is made after the night of prayer, and they go out to their mighty responsible work under the canopy of a Redeemer's night-long supplication to God. In the course of his ministry another and very different experience rises before him. For some purpose, not directly revealed—perhaps to strengthen the faith of his disciples in himself by disclosing to them some of his essential glories; perhaps to strengthen his own heart by some transcendent communion with the heavenly world—for some great purpose he is to be transfigured before the disciples and before the wondering, adoring ages. But he passes under the great change through the gates of prayer. *"As he prayed, the fashion of his counte-*

nance was altered." Drawing near the close of his ministry, when the hour and the meaning of his great sacrifice press themselves upon his soul with so marvelous distinctness and poignancy, he exclaims, "Now is my soul troubled, and what shall I say?" And he answers his own question by a prayer to his Father in heaven.

At last the ministry is drawing to its close. The last supper is celebrated; the last discourses are uttered. His teaching mounts to its sublimest reach and stretches to its utmost range. As he began his public ministry by prayer so must it be closed in prayer; and thus was breathed forth the last, the intercessory prayer of Christ, which rises into a grandeur of supplication so subdued, so tender, that it is the very holy of holies of inspiration. These all were emergencies of labor, emergencies of suffering. How fruitful in every age have they not been in evoking from human lips plaintive, passionate cries to Heaven. We look into the shades of Gethsemane, and see stretched out in dim outline beneath the olive trees the prostrate Son of God. We hear a prayer; it struggles up into utterance, every word palpitating with a great anguish. Thrice—thrice it smites our ears and pierces the heavens: "Father, if it be possible, let this cup pass from me." The cup did not pass, but an angel came. And then, oh then, in the supreme moment, when the sacrifice was complete and redemption was finished, once more Christ prayed, "Father, into thy hands I commend my spirit," and his life went out in the breathing of a prayer. Olivet, Hermon, Gethsemane, Calvary—what views they give us of the praying Christ! These emergencies of his history fall, as you perceive, into two classes. They are emergencies of labor or suffering. Either he has some vaster responsibilities to meet, or his soul is to pass under the baptism of some great anguish, and in both he needs to pray, in both does pray, and teaches us how to pray in both. In just those periods, at just those points of his life when sacred destinies are most densely gathered, those passages in his history on which, therefore, the gaze of men would be most intensely fixed, there we find him praying. So do Christ's prayers lie at the very heart of his ministry. His devotional habits were marked by the two great traits of intensity and perseverance. He who taught that men ought always to pray and not to faint, rose up a great while before day and departed into a solitary place, and there prayed, or spent a night of solitude in supplication. Prayer was no occasional, sporadic element in Christ's life. The fountain leaping far into the air shows the deeply hidden spring; and so prayer comes to the forefront in the life of Christ. Side by side with teachings, with deeds, with sufferings which proclaim him the God incarnate, the man divine, Christ's prayers show what celestial forces played through that life, finding it so perfectly human in its experiences of want, and making it so perfectly divine in its blessedness of supply. Still we must advance one step farther and see how Christ's prayerfulness was balanced by Christ's laboriousness.

It has not always been the case that so-called men of prayer have been men of Christian toil. Much, indeed, of so-called communion with God seems to be an end in itself, looking to enjoyment or to a sort of spiritual development, which is pietism, but not piety. The mystics of the Middle Ages, like John Tauler, some more modern mystics, like Madame Guyon, approached dangerously near such an error, if they did not topple over its verge. There is an ignorant piety full of emotionalism, which is fluent in prayer, works itself up into a sort of ecstasy, but which has apparently no moral basis. But without going at length into these fearful distortions of true prayerfulness, which shock and disgust all right-minded people, skeptics and intelligent believers alike, we may find some food for thought in the great disparity for many of us between the amount of our praying and the amount of our working. How often we have prayed with undoubted fervor and sincerity for the kingdom of God! If by an effort of memory we could recall the numbers of such prayers *we* have offered, and if by any disclosure we could see the numbers of prayers the saints of all ages have offered, and could compare them with the actual labors put forth, manifold as these have been, we should be overwhelmed with the enormous disparity between praying and working. It is so easy to pray, and so hard to work—that is, it is so easy to go through the motions or forms of prayer; but to work—there comes the test of courage, endurance, faith. To say, "Thy kingdom come," and to feel that it would be so blessed and so glorious if it only would come, this is surely no thorny path to tread. But to translate the prayer into action, to do the deed on which the coming kingdom depends, "ay, there's the rub."

The moment, however, we look at prayer as it stands in the life of any saint of God, Old Testament or New, that moment we see no such disparity existing. Every man of prayer is a man of toil too. Elijah prayed, and the heavens gave no rain. Again he prayed, and the heavens gave forth the rain abundantly. He was a man of like passions as we are. But look at that stern, mighty old prophet, majestic figure that he is, of uncompromising fidelity in a time of apostasy, and see how in him mighty labors kept even pace with mighty prayers. The same thing is true of Paul. His simple but appealing words show us the man, whose very conversion was heralded by the words, "Behold, he prayeth." "*Night and day praying exceedingly for you.*" But all this life of devotion, how it rises against a mighty background of toil and suffering for his Lord.

In Christ, however, most conspicuously are the two elements joined—the praying and the working. Paint his devotional life in never so vivid colors, his working life keeps in harmony with every tint and outline. In fact, what gives this picture in the text—Christ praying alone on the mountain-top through the long night-watches—its great power and glory is that he went to that mountain-top after one day of toil, and would come down from it to engage in another exactly like it; so that if a disciple could say of his unrecorded works, the world itself could not contain the books that might be written to record them, it might also be said that those works of Jesus, so incessant, so numberless, so gracious, are only the outgrowth of an answering prayerfulness. Nor can we duly estimate the prayerfulness of Christ till we look at his prayers as intercessory prayers.

The intercession of Christ is one divine function of his priestly office. He is now fulfilling it, at the right hand of God. One design certainly of the Epistle to the Hebrews is to acquaint us with the nature and the blessedness of the sacerdotal ministry now exercised by Christ in behalf of his people. It must differ from his atoning work. That is finished—complete. It must rest upon and depend on the atoning work, for that is urged as the ground of his intercession. Whatever it is in nature or manifestation, it fills heaven with praise and earth with blessing. Now, of this heavenly intercession some of his earthly supplications are beautiful types. Indeed, in one sense, as his whole life was vicarious, so all his praying is vicarious. If it was in form prayer a blessing to himself, it is in fact prayer that he might thereby bless the world he came to redeem. But his prayers often assumed directly the intercessory form and style. As such, they interpret to us what are the heavenly intercessions within the veil still offered for his people. Young children were brought to him that he should put his hands upon them and *pray.* "And he took them up in his arms, put his hands upon them, and blessed them." Christ praying for a group of children—does this seem to any mind a lowly office for him to assume? If so, it is only because the question of childhood is feebly conceived and its immense range overlooked, or because the blessed truth is unappreciated that the very greatness of divine love is often manifest in the feebleness and helplessness of the objects toward which it is exercised. When, a generation since, a gifted Christian poetess wrote her "Cry of the Children," the Christian world was roused by her pathetic, indignant song. What was it, after all, but a faint echo from a Christian woman's soul of what ages before had been heard in Palestine, when Christ made *his* prayer for childhood?

Still more specifically and powerfully does Christ commend to our hearts the intercessory type of prayer in his words to the apostle Peter: "And the Lord said, Simon, Simon, behold, Satan hath desired to have you, that he may sift you as wheat: but I have prayed for thee, that thy faith fail not." Christ knew this disciple stood in imminent peril; that his soul would shortly be shaken in gusts of temptation, "as when one thresheth wheat upon the threshing floor and winnoweth it." The story of Simon Peter's denial of his Lord is the actual commentary on this word of the Lord. What kept him safe in that terrible hour from final, utter apostasy? What saved him from a shipwreck of faith, hopeless, irretrievable, disastrous? That intercession of Christ—that, and that alone. "I have prayed for thee, that thy faith fail not." There was evidently an hour when Jesus bore in prayer to his Father the case of this imperiled disciple, when Christ pleaded for him at the throne of grace, and forever illustrated for all men and all time the great doctrine of intercession. It is only, however, when we turn to Christ's last or intercessory prayer, recorded in the seventeenth chapter of St. John's Gospel, that we can grasp any fit conception of what Christ's earthly intercessions were for fullness and richness. What vastness of range, as it covers the whole body of the faithful, that great multitude which no man can number, gathered from the east and the west, the north and the south, and who stood to Christ as all those who had been given him! What ages of Christian toil and Christian conflict, suffering and testimony, self-sacrifice and aspiration, it covers, as the one body of Christian discipleship is brought under the terms of this prayer! What richness, what amplitude of petition, as it stretches away from sanctification on earth to glorification in heaven, from holy ward against the evil that is in the world, to participation and so perception of the glory which Christ has and had before the foundation of the world. As his miracles are the fit symbols of his power, so this intercessory prayer is the fit symbol of his intercessions in heaven, interpreting and endearing them to our human hearts as we slowly and painfully struggle upward along the path of Christian discipline, sorrow, and toil.

And thus, indeed, are we brought to see the fact that Christ, in these prayers of an earthly intercession, reveals to us the moral grandeur as well as preciousness there is in prayer. If a man could only pray for himself, if by some limitation in the nature of things, or in the immutable sovereignty of God, every soul had the privilege for itself alone, even then such a boon offered to all were a priceless blessing. But now, as intercession for others, how prayer rises and swells into moral grandeur and moral worth! Jesus, standing with his disciples about the table on which the sacrament of the last supper was yet to be celebrated, and as they were about to start for the garden across the brook Kedron, lifts his eyes to heaven. But he has already looked down through the ages, far across continents then unknown, and sees the fast gathering throng of his disciples; sees them toiling, witnessing, suffering for his sake; sees the faithful leaders in one generation die, and those of the next run to take their places; sees all the dreadful corruptions, all the stern conflicts, all the sad heresies and schisms, all the triumphs too, and growths, as the blessed leaven slowly leavens the whole lump; and as he looks on the whole up to the very end, he prays for all those who should believe on him through the word of his apostles. And from this scene on earth we look reverently up to his throne in heaven, where he ever liveth to make intercession for us.

This study of Christ's devotional habits leads straight to several lessons touching on vital spiritual interests. First, as to the individual, we can see how large a place prayer ought to hold in every human life. Did Jesus Christ find such need of prayer? Was he in his sinless manhood so beset by duties and pressed by responsibilities and sorrows that *he* had need of this strong crying and tears? We may be sure that he who was the Truth prayed because prayer met, and prayer only could meet, actual, living, daily wants. But if this is true for Christ, how much more for men, who are sinful and weak and ignorant. What an awful vacuum is a prayerless life! There is not a soul before me, not one, but is so encompassed with infirmities, and yet has so much of Christian responsibility in one shape or other to meet; but is so poorly equipped for service of Christ, compared with what he should be as a servant of the Lord; but has so many and so pressing spiritual wants, that if such a life be prayerless, it is a moral anomaly baffling all explanation, save that which comes in an unbelieving and hardened heart. In fact, it is the privilege of man to pray, because we have a Mediator with God—Christ Jesus. Prayer, then, in human life, by reason of its needs so manifold and pressing, by reason of its perils so various and so imminent, by reason of its opportunities so gracious and so fleeting—prayer ought to come to the front in every man's life as a spiritual power, a power with God. Thus it stands in the life of Christ. Thus he has put it for all men by his own divine example. Effectual and fervent praying may sound depths, as it may test qualities of manhood, which working never can.

Secondly, as to the body of Christian discipleship. For as an agency in promoting the kingdom of God on earth, prayer is to be put, not side by side with the preaching of the Word and ordinances, but above them. They are nothing except a divine influence vitalizes them, and that divine influence the power of the Spirit of God, that comes only along the channels opened by prayer. So Christ, in the model of all prayer, taught his disciples to say, "Thy kingdom come."

Prayer as an agency for promoting the kingdom of God is prayer in its form of intercession. It has all the moral grandeur and all the divine tenderness which are reflected from Christ's prayer for the believers of all ages. And the danger which now more than any other threatens us is that we shall be found looking away from the sole efficacious element in spiritual growth, the might of God's Spirit, to what is adventitious, subordinate—to the mere instrument, to the "drawing element" in the pulpit, to the "live element" in the prayer-meeting, to the blackboard element in the Sunday-school, to the thousand and one expedients devised for making religion interesting; whereas, if we did but remember it, one breath of God's spirit on a human soul, one touch of that Spirit on the long-sealed spiritual vision, and the whole soul is alert and absorbed by the great spiritual interests, by truth, by the means of grace. No need now for the spicery of religious entertainments. The soul has come to find in the sober, earnest following of Christ what expands all its powers and meets all its wants. While this age, as all ages past, can forget the ancient warning, "*Cursed is the man that maketh an arm of flesh his trust*," only at deadly peril and unutterable loss, there is this difference between Christ's praying and our own. He always prayed aright; we ask amiss. And we enter into the secret of Christ's praying only as we pray to our heavenly Father above all fear of violating natural laws, and in the perfect confidence that God can answer any wise prayer, and have the whole system of laws move majestically forward, untroubled as the slumber of an infant. "Thinkest thou that I cannot now pray to my Father, and he shall presently give me twelve legions of angels?" This was the faith of Jesus in prayer, that by the opening of his lips in a supplication he could fill the sky above him with twelve legions of angels, hovering above his head, a canopy of defense from all harm, and filling the air with their shining squadrons. This should be our faith in prayer, that it will bring into our lives and into the lives of others, unnumbered and matchless blessings which will never come unless our lips open to pray. Cure your doubts about prayer by looking to Jesus. Philosophy will not cure them, but the example of a praying Christ may and can cure your weakness of faith in prayer by recalling the sincerity and strength of Christ's confidence in it, and its manifest answers in his history. Come into his theory of prayer, and it shall cease to wear any tentative, experimental look. It shall be a power with God.

Rebuke all your bad habits as to prayer, all your indolence in and suppression of prayer, by this study of the devotional habits of Christ, not as an abstraction in theological science, but as a lifelike thing in the history of Jesus. Put no more excuses before God for your meagerness in prayer because of your distracted life. Learn from Jesus how to bring the calming influences of prayer into the distractions of your business. Seek, as he sought, every outward aid to prayer: stillness of night-seasons, freshness of morning dawn, solitude of sequestered places. Then shall prayer in your life rise to the majesty and worth of its office—as communion with Heaven.

THE TRANSFIGURATION OF LIFE BY CHRIST.

BY PROF. JAMES O. MURRAY, D.D., LL.D.

"*And as he prayed, the fashion of his countenance was altered, and his raiment was white and glistening.*"—LUKE 9:29.

THERE are two ways of looking at the Transfiguration of our Lord, or rather two lights in which the wonderful incident may be viewed. One reflects it simply as related in its scope and meaning to the person of our Saviour, and to some teaching upon his character and work. In this view it has connection with Christian life only as that life is interested in any disclosure of our Lord's glory. The broader and deeper conception sees in it all this, and besides this, the truth that in Christ everything is transfigured for a Christian. As we are taught that the splendors of his transfiguration reached even to his garments, and while the fashion of his countenance was altered and did shine as the sun, his raiment became exceeding white as snow, so as no fuller on earth could whiten it, so the transfiguration of Christ spreads over and touches with heavenly glories whatever he dwells in. For his name is Emmanuel—God with us. "The Word was made flesh and dwelt among us." The whole mount was transformed by the bright overshadowing cloud. Even the disciples caught some of the reflected glories, and longed to abide there. An adoring and simple Christian faith delights to see, therefore, in this scene a symbolic teaching as well as a transcendent historic fact in the life of Jesus. That teaching is, our Lord transfigures life for his disciples, sets their whole human earthly existence in new lights. The incarnate Saviour was *so* glorified, that we might understand that he has power to shed transfiguration-glories over that life in which he came down from heaven to take part. I shall try to show how he can do this, and actually does do this for many a Christian soul, by unfolding various human experiences as thus transfigured in Christ.

First, then, look at earthly cares in this new transfiguring light which may shine on them from Hermon. Subtracting at once from daily life all its *unnecessary* cares, those made by our artificial and foolish wants, by our pride or by our inordinate, racing ambitions, the actual burden of necessary cares is very great. Those belonging to man in his sphere, and to woman in hers, household cares and business cares, sacred as the home can make them, severe and engrossing as business life exacts, all such absorb our time, tax our energies and our patience and our skill, and seemingly enter into life as its controlling element. Other burdens come into life as occasions. Their pressure is intermittent. These are constant. Their pressure is never lifted. I do not see that wealth seems to make much difference in the matter, for though apparently it has the power to purchase exemption from much that is wearisome, it has its own burdens to carry. The world is full of careworn faces among rich and poor, and where the face may be unwrinkled yet the heart is careworn. There is no social science that can rid us of these cares of life. They are in it by divine appointment for a discipline of character. The noblest type of life has them most characteristically in it. For civilized life differs from savage life; among many other things, prominently in this, that it sees and assumes the legitimate and real burdens of care which God has assigned to life, and only by seeing and assuming which our human life can advance to its completeness for the individual, for society, for the state, and for the Church.

Yet in a *worldly* or a *stoical*—that is, an unspiritual, unchristlike—way of looking at this feature of our existence, it resolves itself into so much *drudgery*. It makes up a large part of what are called the "*worries*" of life. The energies and the patience and the skill are gathered up to encounter them, because the livelihood or the bodily comfort, or at best the fortune or the competence which is to purchase exemption from them, lies at the end of the road dragging itself wearily and roughly through them. How welcome is sometimes the slumber at the close of a day full of such ceaseless drudgeries, in which for a few hours they are buried in a welcome oblivion! How cheerless, vexatious, harassing is the night season in which these drudgeries are laid on sleepless pillows, where they hold a witches' dance before the unwilling but compelled imagination in distorted shapes!

It seems also to make little difference as to the relative dignity of these cares of life. If men high in stations of public life told all they knew of its drudgeries, something of its glamour would certainly vanish. It is simply nobler drudgery than what falls to the lot of the hodcarrier or the washerwoman. Now, if there is no way by which all such earthly drudgeries can be transfigured, brought into some new light, and made even to shine with some heavenly radiance, then for by far the greater part of mankind and womankind the moil and toil of life are hard, dull, oppressive realities, from which there are occasional brief respites, yet which make the work, the daily occupation a stern, stubborn necessity, and that is all the account to give of it.

There is, however, a transfiguration for such cares. If they are viewed as part of a wise and gracious Christian discipline for character; if they are made the educators of Christian courage, Christian patience, Christian gentleness, Christian calmness, Christian submission, they are set in a new light as means of grace. As the attraction of gravitation is as much a law of God as the first commandment in the Decalogue, so this means of grace in the ordered discipline of life, through its cares, transfigures the cares from drudgeries into the ministers of Christ. All this will be missed, however, if instead of looking at them as means of grace they are thought of and treated as hindrances to grace. A mountain, unless you climb it, may shut out your view. Transfigure the cares of life into means of grace, surround them with that holy light which Christ sheds on them as daily discipline of character in us—of character according to his teaching and example—and you will find that if life has its Gethsemanes for us all it has

THE TRANSFIGURATION OF LIFE BY CHRIST. 217

also its Hermons. Counting-rooms and nurseries may as well be Bethels of the soul as was the city of Luz to the patriarch. But before many men and women see them as such they will have to awake out of sleep, saying, "Surely the Lord *is* in these places, and we knew it not."

The transfiguration of life for us by Christ sweeps over a broader field, however, for, *secondly, the sorrows of life* can in the same way be transfigured through him.

"Perhaps," said Vinet, "to suffer is nothing else than to live more deeply. *Love* and *sorrow* are the two conditions of a profound life. Woe to him who should be without affliction here below—whom the divine Educator should have excluded from his mysterious school! We might well ask ourselves at sight of so alarming a felicity, 'What has he done to be thus overlooked? Is he too pure to be passed through the crucible, or too bad, too desperate, to be worth trying there?'"

Sorrow is, indeed, in one form or another, as inevitable as death itself. It is a poor life which has not known grief in some form. It is a cheap and superficial and vulgar conception of life which craves an existence untouched by suffering, whose best symbol would be a rocking-chair or a bed of down. For there come down to us from the serene heights of inspiration these tender and sacred words applied to the *one spotless* human life: "Though he were a Son, yet learned he obedience by the things that he suffered." Never was truer word spoken by mortal man than that word of Vinet, "Love and sorrow are the two conditions of a profound life." They find at once their mighty proof and their transcendent illustration in the life of the "Man of Sorrows." For surely it is the profound and awful meaning of Gethsemane, as the prelude to the divine Sacrifice, that there love and sorrow meet and mingle in an eternal consecrated mystery.

And yet there is a way of looking at human sorrows which denudes them of all dignity and depth of meaning. If I see in them only so much pain of wounded sensibilities shooting its fiery darts into the soul, only so much anguish to be hidden away from the sight of one's fellows, as the wounded animal leaves the herd to die; if the woes which come soon or late are so much inevitable grief put into my earthly lot by operation of laws or by the environments of the great system, and to be simply accepted and stoically borne; if the very best thing, the only wise and true thing to be said and done for a sorrowful spirit is to speak to it kindly in some warm and tender human sympathy, and commit it to the healing tendencies of time—then this sorrowful side of human existence, which is so large a part of it, so dark a part of it, so painful and prolonged a part of it, becomes all that the pessimism of Schopenhauer or Hartmann has ever painted it, and what one had better do is just to keep his eyes from seeing it, until he has to see it and feel it for himself. If anything in life needs transfiguration it is surely human sorrow.

It finds such in Christ. It is not so much heartache, so much mental anguish, so much unmet longing, so shadowing and depressing gloom, "crushing us back and imprisoning ourselves" in our own dark forebodings; it is a discipline of character through which we can grow into choice Christian graces, and through which as its last and fullest achievement we can even grow into fellowship with Christ's sufferings; by which on the one hand we are made humble, gentle, patient, unselfish, and on the other are brought in closer and tenderer relations with Christ Jesus—the Man of Sorrows, the divine Sufferer. "Always to suffer, yet always to love, would be paradise in comparison with always prospering and always hating." Who cannot recall to memory some instance of that divinest thing in life—a sanctified sorrow, a holy grief; some silver-haired parent who has passed through deep waters; some dear child whose young, fair life was early touched with the chastening influences of suffering? Placid, chastened, submissive, sympathetic, hopeful, radiant at times with the expectation of heaven, yet grateful for every sweetness yet spared in life, to which the sunniest childhood will in its frolics and mirth betake itself and nestle there, there is no spiritual beauty in life to compare with it. Yet what a transfiguration it is! Out of tears and pains and conflicts it has all come. Just as the light of Christ's transfiguration-glories, glancing on the rocks of Hermon, made them glow as if they were the walls of heaven, so the power of a heavenly, spiritual discipline through Christ and in Christ puts this transfiguration on sorrow. In that glorified form on Hermon Peter and James and John did not see the "Man of Sorrows." They saw a glorified Redeemer, into which he had been transfigured. Philosophy may stoically bear or proudly conceal grief; human sympathy may lightly assuage grief; time may dull grief; but only Christ can transfigure it; and when the sorrows of life have been transmuted into a sweet and gracious spiritual discipline of character, not Hermon itself ever saw a more veritable transfiguration.

THE TRANSFIGURATION OF LIFE BY CHRIST.

Darker clouds than those either of care or sorrow gather above human life—clouds of temptation. Yet, *thirdly*, for this also there is in Christ a transfiguring power.

Most of us live on from day to day taking little note of the large part which temptation plays in our probation. The misjudging comes from not observing the real nature of temptation—that it can come from within as well as from without; that it may be seductively quiet as well as stormily oppressive. A constant strain is put on our supposed or real goodness from three sources. First from within. Every man is tempted when he is drawn away of his own *lust* and enticed. What can this word lust mean here but every sort of unlawful desire? It means the unlawful desire for lawful things as well as for the unlawful objects; for excessive praise as well as for unholy pleasures. It means an inordinate ambition for wealth, power, social distinction, just as much as a gluttony or drunkenness. The heart called "purest" by men has yet its lusts which draw it away and entice it from God. So, too, there are outward conditions in life out of which spring, as wild beasts from hidden lairs, so many solicitations to evil. Business, society, a humdrum life, as well as an absorbing and excited life, all may in turn become temptations, if not to gross and repulsive forms of evil, to worldly, unspiritual lives, and they are as real as any that horrified the soul of St. Anthony in his cave. Of course the range of temptation in outward conditions of life takes a far wider range than the abuse of lawful things; men are tempted by other men, by the general drift of evil, by the success of wicked or doubtful courses, by the ingenious fascinations thrown around sin, and by the acute, ingenious, subtle excuse for it, which is a prominent feature of sinning nowadays.

And then, ah, then! in reserve, lying in wait behind all this inward and outward form of temptation, is solicitation to evil from the adversary of our souls. The devil, I fear, has by many been dismissed to the limbo of exploded fallacies. Nobody seems much afraid of him. It is an amazing and extreme reaction from the belief of those days when Luther flung his inkstand at him. But how solemnly ever the Bible speaks of his power as a tempter! The Bible treats him as no shadowy phantom. And quite possibly the Bible, dealing as it does with this question of human wickedness in its deep and searching way, has quite as much true philosophy on its side as those who, with some airs of enlightened superiority, remand the whole question to nursery tales of ghosts and goblins.

THE TRANSFIGURATION OF LIFE BY CHRIST.

How little we may know *when* we are under his power! Satan himself is transformed into an angel of light. At the very moment when a Christian may be excusing himself for some questionable act, and so deftly that his conscience gives not a note of warning, he may be simply yielding to Satan transformed. He little knows what infernal power of evil lurks in that angel of light.

So compacted, so subtle, so effective is all this triple system of evil, they are a correlative and moral force of prodigious power in life. How shall it be regarded? As a dark and terrible evil host let loose upon man here? As such, is it to be viewed by thoughtful souls as casting a baleful and portentous shadow over every scene in life? Is a troubled and stealthy suspicion to haunt us forever, as we go about in the sweet sunshine and among the blessed companionships of life—a suspicion that every flower has under it the coiled adder? Must a mother feel when her son leaves the home which has so long and so carefully sheltered him that he goes out to live under so fearful a cloud of solicitation to evil, and that nothing is to be said save that it is the grim and obstinate necessity of existence; that it is a somber and fearful mystery of our condition, for which there is not only no explanation, but for which there is no sort of alleviation? Or can this dark cloud turn forth its silver lining on the night?

Assuredly Jesus Christ has put a different face upon temptations. Vanquished in his strength, by the power of his grace they are transfigured. " Blessed is the man," is the voice of his gospel, " that endureth temptation: for when he is tried, he shall receive the crown of life, which the Lord hath promised to them that love him." Seven times in the opening chapters of Revelation does the assurance ring out, " to him that overcometh " shall be given thrones and dominions, palms and scepters. A temptation overcome is thus a temptation transfigured. A solicitation to evil resisted has become a glory to the soul that resisted it. Its darkness has been changed for light; its fiery dart has become a spiritual scepter; its poison has become the hidden manna. Lose not the cheering view which such assurances give by any notion that it is true for great temptations but not for small; true for great conquerors of moral evil, but not for lowly souls struggling in obscurity against some evil habit, some petulant temper, some selfish hardness, some miserable pride, some evil lust. True for one, then true for all. True for Jesus in the desert, true for Jesus' followers in the home, in the street, in the stir of a mighty life, in the silence of an enforced solitude. So Christ lights up for men this whole side of life. It may have its mysteries still, and at times seem an impenetrable cloud. Still light shines on the cloud. It becomes even radiant and golden. Christ transfigures temptation just as he does care and sorrow. He makes of it a discipline out of which come strength, glory, joy. At these solemn junctures of our life his grace comes in—sometimes a shield and buckler, sometimes a flaming sword—and by its might we are made strong to resist evil. Nay, more, at these spiritual crises he himself, tempted once as we are tempted, knowing its anguish, its suspense, its horrors perhaps, is a living Presence with us in the thick of conflict. And thus the transfiguration comes; comes as it came on Hermon of old. We see white-robed saints who have overcome, shining in transfiguration-glories and we hear the voice from the Mount, and can say even of temptation so transfigured by Jesus, "Lord, it is good to be here."

There is yet a fourth transfiguration of life vouchsafed the believer in Christ, which as it comes last of all is mightiest of all. It comes at the close. It is the transfiguration of death into eternal life.

Surely even for manliest and holiest souls there is needed some such transfiguration-light for death. It is not simply the pains of death, though there may be in store for us long and acute anguish. It is not simply the decay and chill of the grave, though every soul that ever heard or read them must have beat sympathetically with Claudio's when, as great Shakespeare voiced for all time and all men the instinctive shrinking, he said:

> "Ay, but to die, and go we know not where;
> To lie in cold obstruction, and to rot;
> This sensible warm motion to become
> A kneaded clod . . .
>   . . . 'tis too horrible!
> The weariest and most loathed worldly life
> That age, ache, penury, or imprisonment
> Can lay on nature, is a paradise
> To what we fear of death."

It is not the violent wrench from a fond, familiar life where we are at home in the body, from the beautiful world we live in and love. It is not simply the entrance upon a state of being to all whose conditions we are the utterest strangers, of which we have heard so little from out the silences of inspiration on the great theme. It is not the moral idea in death, as the curse of sin, to which we all must bow. It is all this combined and united with the instinctive clinging to life, which it takes so terrible experiences of pain or misery or wildest manias to overcome, it is all of this put together which makes thoughtful souls in bondage all their lives long through fear of death. I know there is a naturalistic philosophy which affects indifference to the subject, treating it simply as the wearing out of a machine, or the burning out of the fire. I know there is a fatalistic way of looking at the subject which affects to be unmoved by it since the hour is fixed, cannot be hastened, cannot be delayed. I know, on the other hand, that some Christian hymns are pitched in a key of sentimentalism on this great subject, which virtually treats death as if it were less than the amputation of a limb by the surgeon's knife. For myself, all I can say is I cannot quite get to this high pitch. I must modulate my thinking in a lower key, and in that low and deep refrain of an ancient psalmist say: "Make me to know mine end, and the measure of my days what it is; that I may know how frail I am."

Yet there is a transfiguration for death which comes through Christ. It comes first of all in that full clear revelation of immortality which the world had for the first time when Christ brought life and immortality to light through his Gospel. Nothing shows the advance of New upon Old Testament teaching like this. It is the advance of mid-noon upon twilight. Nothing shows the advance of New Testament revelation upon all philosophy more than this. Here it is the advance of reality upon conjecture, or of certainty upon probability, or of personal knowledge upon hopes or expectations. For a clear, bright, blessed revelation of immortality instantly transfigures death. Then it is not the be-all and the end-all here. Then it is not annihilation, not decay and nothingness. There is beyond it the light of life, the life eternal. That light transfigures death.

We may not stop here. Christ's revelation is not merely general. He has had a few things to say about the great theme. Few as they are, they change the whole aspect of the subject. If we had only his words at the grave of Lazarus, it would be enough to make death luminous forever with strange, unearthly light. Jesus said to Martha, "I am the resurrection, and the life: he that believeth in me, though he were dead, yet shall he live: and whosoever liveth and believeth in me shall never die. Believest thou this?" If you can say with Martha, "Yea, Lord, I believe," then is death transfigured into life.

But a more subduing because a more familiar and closer teaching of his is found in his words to the disciples: "In my Father's house are many mansions." And here, what gives these few simple words their marvelous power to light

THE TRANSFIGURATION OF LIFE BY CHRIST.

up this great subject of the future existence is his added word of assurance, "If it were not so, I would have told you." There is an artless simplicity here which is unique in the teaching of Christ. What an appeal to the confidence of his followers! I could better part with any of his miracles than with these few words, on which Christ has staked his simple truthfulness. "If it were not so, I would have told you." If what were not so? Why, if his disciples were not to be in his Father's house, and if he were not to receive them to himself as one by one they passed from death into life.

And yet we do not enter into the fullness of Christ's transfiguration of death till his own resurrection from the dead has been thoroughly meditated. Not as the crowning proof of his divine ministry and sacrifice. It *is* an evidence of Christianity which has been the bulwark against which every wave of skepticism has dashed and broken. But it is vastly more than this. It is the holy certitude that his followers rise with him into the eternal glory. In his resurrection, that of believers is contained as pledge and prophecy. So St. Paul mainly teaches us in that sublime reach of inspired truth given us in the fifteenth chapter of First Corinthians, which comes to its climax of meaning and of glorious joy in his outburst, "Death is swallowed up in victory." Nor, indeed, do we reach the completeness of meaning in the resurrection of Christ till we couple with it that posthumous ministry of forty days. The two are parts of one divine whole. How divinely that ministry teaches us that death has not sundered the old relations! Christ takes them up again. That soul-subduing interview with Thomas, that fruitful and tender dealing with Peter by the shore of the lake, how luminous with the blessed assurance that death has no power to uproot the affections and the warm, sweet relations of our human earthly life! Had Hermon a mightier and more sacred transfiguration than this? Nay, is it not the glory of Hermon's transfiguration that it proclaims forever the interest of departed saints in the scenes now enacting on earth? For Moses and Elias spake with him of the decease he should shortly accomplish at Jerusalem. What was death to Moses as then and there he spake with Christ? It was the memory, dim and distant, of a brief struggle. It was the shining gate through which he had passed in the solitude of Nebo to the society and blessedness of heaven. It was the transfiguration of a bitter disappointment in not seeing the earthly Canaan into the fulfillment of a more glorious hope—the beatific vision of the heavenly Canaan. And so Christ transfigures death. The curse for sin—it is swallowed up in victory. The mortal pang—it becomes the everlasting felicity. The departure from this life—it is the entrance upon life eternal.

Yet most evidently such transfiguration of life's cares and sorrows have not come to all disciples. It lies among the unrealized possibilities of Christian experience. It has its own method. It is reached in one way, by one process of spiritual life. How, then, may life thus be transfigured for me in Christ, so that under all its burdens, and amid all its sorrows and temptations, and in full view of the grave which awaits me at its close, I may yet always be the glad disciple, my whole soul radiant with joy in the existence here? The text points out the secret of this marvelous result. How did Christ's own transfiguration come about? "As he prayed, the fashion of his countenance was altered." *As he prayed.* It seems to be implied in this that it was no sudden outburst of glory from the opened gates of heaven, but a gradual envelopment and transformation while he was praying. It was nightfall. Silence was in the heavens above and on the hills around. And in that silence and darkness Christ began his communion with God. The longing is irrepressible to know what this prayer of Jesus covered, what petitions, what blessed fellowship with his Father. But all we know is that as he prayed and his soul was more and more rapt in his heavenly communion, the transcendent scene began, at first all unnoticed by his disciples; and then, as the strange, unearthly light began stealing over Jesus and the mountain-top, and the fashion of his countenace was altered, his garments glistening more and more, the fullness of transfiguration-glory is reached in the appearance of Moses and Elias with him on that Mount of a more splendid theophany than ever had gleamed from the Shekinah of old. The transfiguration came to Christ in prayer. So if life is ever transfigured from its hard, dull reality, its burdens and woes, its secret griefs or coming shadows, into any deep, glad, spiritual meaning, and the glory of Christ shines down into our very sorrows and temptations, it will be because we have learned how to pray in some deep devotion, in some holy altitude of spiritual retirement. Was not life transfigured for the Psalmist when tears had been his meat day and night, when all God's waves and billows had gone over him, yet when in the voice of holy psalm he could say, "Why art thou cast down, O my soul? and why art thou disquieted within me? Hope thou in God: for I shall yet praise him, who is

THE TRANSFIGURATION OF LIFE BY CHRIST. 233

the health of my countenance, and my God." Was not life transfigured for Paul when, under the heavy burden of an unknown and tormenting agony, he besought the Lord thrice that it might depart from him, and came to say at length, "Most gladly, therefore, will I glory in my infirmities." Infirmity, anguish, changed into glory. The secret of the matter lies in this, prayer puts things for us in new light. We see through prayer what else were hidden from our sight. It is heavenly light. And then in us, as in the person of Christ, the change comes too. We see with new eyes—eyes of faith and love and submission and hope. So has Trench sung in a choice Christian sonnet:

> "Lord, what a change within us one short hour
> Spent in thy presence will avail to make'
> What heavy burdens from our bosoms take!
> What parched fields refresh as with a shower!
> We kneel, and all around us seems to tower;
> We rise, and all, the distant and the near,
> Stands forth in sunny outlines brave and clear.
> We kneel, how weak; we rise, how full of power!"

O Christian, if thou wouldst have more of such transfigurations in life, seek them in prayer. Let Hermon take its place in your Christian experience. Without such a transfiguration, life, and life made the most and best of, will only prove fantastic mockery, as well as fearful mystery. It will be all that pessimism paints it for delusion and woe. It will be what Macbeth said it was to him in his hour of crime and desolation:

"... A tale
Told by an idiot, full of sound and fury,
Signifying nothing."

But with such a transfiguration, life with all its cares and sorrows and temptations, its woes and aches and death, becomes an existence measureless in its possibilities of disciplined character, exalted service, exuberant gladness, immortal hopes, and finally eternal fruition.

CHRISTIAN MANLINESS.*

BY PROF. WILLIAM HENRY GREEN, D.D, LL.D.

"*Quit you like men.*"—1 COR. 16 : 13.

IT was the habit of the Apostle Paul to crown the doctrinal discussion in the body of his epistles with a practical application at the end, in which he urged upon his readers the obligations involved in the doctrines which they had been considering. This suggests the propriety of a like practical application to ourselves of the studies in which we have been engaged during the seminary year that is now closing. The Apostle in the text sums up for us in a single word the deduction to be made alike from the theological, the biblical, the historical, and the ecclesiastical studies which we have been pursuing—ἀνδρίζεσθε, *Quit you like men.*

An injunction to men to act as men seems singular at first view. How else could they act? How can they be anything but what they are? Every substance in the universe is what it is, and

---

* Preached on the closing Sabbath of the seminary term.

acts agreeably to the laws of its being. Every atom of oxygen acts uniformly as oxygen. Every plant and every animal is obedient to the law of its constitution. How, then, can it be necessary to enjoin it upon men to be men and to quit themselves like men?

There are two reasons for this. In the first place man is not, like the inferior creation, subject to the control of physical necessity. Inanimate nature is under a constraint which binds it to unvarying uniformity of action; the specific properties of matter assert themselves with endless constancy. The lower animals are governed by their native instinct; they are led by blind impulse to do what their nature requires. Man is possessed of reason and of choice. No invariable force determines for him the employment of his powers or the direction of his life. If he would be a man indeed, he must make this his definite aim and must employ suitable endeavors. He must by a faithful course of self-discipline develop his powers to the full and in the right direction; and he must by their skillful use attain to the mastery and proper handling of them if he would make of himself what he is meant to be, and what he is capable of becoming. Since this is a result which does not follow of itself, and is only to be attained, if at all, by seeking and toiling, it is well that he should be reminded of what is herein dependent upon himself.

And, in the second place, it is still more requisite that this should be done when we remember the influences that are at work within him and around him to degrade his nature and to frustrate the end of his existence. The corruption inherited from the fall has perverted his faculties and turned them away from their true end. The temptations and solicitations which beset him on every hand bewilder and confuse his mind, and create an eager appetite for everything but that which he should desire and strive after. The aim of the text is to break the spell of this unworthy fascination by reminding men of their true nature and capabilities, that thus, instead of sinking to the level of what is so far beneath them, they may, if possible, be induced to "quit themselves like men."

The appeal of the text addresses itself to all, and is of the most powerful and stimulating character. It is no arbitrary requirement to which you are exhorted to submit. It is nothing alien and uncongenial, as though you were bidden to put on some outlandish garb or wear some ill-fitting dress which offended your sense of propriety or hampered the free movement of your limbs. Nor does it simply urge the claims of duty, the abstract law of right, what ought to be done at whatever sacrifice of inclination. But it may be expected to enlist every human sympathy, and to bring to its aid every generous impulse, since its summons is that you should be true to yourself and to your own nature. Evoke your dormant energies; put forth the powers that are within you; stifle not the noble emotions that stir your breast; act up to your real capacity; fulfill your own high conceptions and aspirations; achieve results worthy of yourself, such as you can review with satisfaction and expose to others without shame. The text bids you to be thus a law to yourself. With what a charge you have been intrusted in being made a free agent—a charge that you can neither surrender nor evade! How vast and unimagined is that which has been put within your own control in your being made master of yourself! What noble faculties, what fine susceptibilities, what magnificent opportunities, what possibilities of high achievement, what ends may be attained, what acquisitions made, what treasures amassed, what a destiny secured, if you will but quit yourselves like men!

It adds to the power of this appeal that it is also adapted to provoke a generous emulation, and that upon the broadest and most comprehensive scale. It is not limited to that which concerns ourselves merely as individuals, but is addressed to the nature which we possess in common with the whole human race. In bidding us to quit ourselves like men it arrays before us all that men are and have been, all that they can do and have done; everything in the character or conduct of any of our fellow-men that kindles enthusiasm or deserves our admiration; all that is wise and good and noble and brave; every worthy enterprise, every deed of heroism or of philanthropy; patient toil, unselfish love, gentle, thoughtful kindness, upright discharge of duty, firm adherence to the right, every exhibition of manly qualities in any department of human action, on any plane of life, on whatever scale of magnitude, in great things or in small, conspicuous or unobserved—all is here gathered up in one mighty argument and set before us for our imitation.

An appeal is sometimes pointed by comparison with inferior natures. Men are shamed out of their inactivity by the direction, Go to the ant, thou sluggard; and out of their stupid disregard of their Creator by the reflection that the ox knoweth his owner; and out of their inconsideration by the fact that the stork in the heaven knoweth her appointed times. But there is a reproach inseparable from such an argument, and an implied censure, which, while it goads to duty, nevertheless leaves a sting. There is no such damaging implication when the text would rouse us to a sense of what we may become or what we may achieve by the thought of what others of our own species have shown themselves able to attain or to perform.

It has its advantage also over appeals which are sometimes made with great power to particular classes: as when they who are entering into battle are bidden to demean themselves like soldiers; or they who are set to conduct a nation's affairs to act like statesmen; or they who are engaged in pecuniary transactions to behave like honest men; or they who are in a position to reflect honor or discredit upon their country to remember that they are Americans. The argument of the text loses none of the stimulus of these more special appeals and abates nothing of their urgency, but embraces them all with undiminished cogency within itself; and, gathering the full impetus that is to be derived from every quarter, directs its entire concentrated energy upon the line of each individual life. It is not only from those whose course is parallel to our own that we are to derive an impulse, those who move in the same sphere or in similar circumstances, who are engaged in kindred pursuits or have common aims; the appeal is to the sentiment of a common human nature. Everything that reveals the capabilities of that nature, wherever it may be found, has its meaning and its force for me. The peasant may teach the prince; the child may give a lesson to the man of hoary hairs, the untutored savage to the sage. Admirable qualities shown anywhere within the range of human experience suggest to us that the same may be transplanted into our lives, and may be exhibited only with altered circumstances and conditions in our daily walk. Martyrs and heroes, the good and the great of every age and of every clime, were of the same stock and possessed the same humanity with ourselves. They show the stuff of which we were made; and they call upon us to be in our particular line of life what they were in theirs.

And even misdirected powers show a nature splendid in its ruins, which, if the perversion were removed, might well engender a holy emulation. Zeal misguided is still zeal, which would have been praiseworthy if balanced and mollified by love and shown in the cause of truth. Toils endured and sacrifices made for ignoble ends may rouse to vigorous effort those who are laboring with higher aims. Thus, we may learn lessons of honor from shame, wisdom from folly, virtue from vice, the right use of faculties from their prostitution and abuse. We may bow to the banner that is here uplifted, even when we see it trailing in the dust; and in the picture that is all soiled and begrimed we may discover the strength and the beauty that lie hidden under the foul stains which deface it.

And the universality of the appeal made in the text is attended with another consequence, which further enhances its value. It embraces within its scope the whole range of human obligation. It is not directed merely to some one specific duty or class of duties. This one injunction includes within it all that is incumbent at all times, under all circumstances, and in every relation. Act as men; do what your nature summons you to do. It sets before us as the standard and measure of our duty not merely what is peculiar to ourselves individually, nor merely what has been in actual fact exemplified by others, but the totality of human nature—man as he was made by his Creator, and as he was fitted and designed to be.

If we should put together all the capabilities that men have ever shown, and all the excellences that they have exhibited, all that men have ever done that is worthy of imitation, this would indeed cover a very wide range, and a most exalted mark would thus be set before us. But if there be any capacity in human nature that has never yet found full expression, if there be any reserve of force that has not been brought into adequate and thorough employment, and especially if any damage has infected our nature, or any paralysis come over its powers, so that at its best it falls sadly below its primal estate and fails to reveal itself in its genuine and native character, then the charge of the text reaches back of these impaired faculties and their enfeebled manifestations to man in the genuine and proper sense, to man in full possession of all that properly belongs to him, man in the full vigor of his original constitution, with his native force unbroken, subject to no weakness nor malady, untainted by sin, his nature undepraved. It is man as he should be, the divine ideal of manhood, which the Apostle would set before us when he bids us, "quit you like men."

The meaning of this exhortation to any person to whom it may be addressed will be chiefly dependent on two things. The first is the conception that he has of manhood. "Quit you like men" in a heroic age would be interpreted as demanding personal bravery; by the sensualist, as summoning to the utmost self-indulgence; by the Stoic, as requiring superiority to adverse circumstances. It means one thing to the rude savage and another to the polished courtier. It means one thing to the materialist, to whom this world is all, and a very different thing to him who has grasped the idea of his immortality. In the mouth of the Apostle it derives its signification from the Christian idea of manhood: man made in the image of God; fallen, indeed, but redeemed; fashioned anew after the likeness of Christ, with all the possibilities that are set before him by the delivering power of the Gospel, the heavenly aids that are afforded, and the glorious destiny that is promised. This is what filled his thoughts when he bid us, "quit you like men."

The second consideration which may modify the meaning of the exhortation before us is the sphere of action referred to and the scope which it affords for manly qualities to display themselves. Human characteristics must have an occasion for their manifestation. Statesmanship cannot be developed at jackstraws. Fortitude cannot be shown when there is nothing to endure, nor courage in a time of profound peace, nor compassion where suffering and want do not exist, nor fidelity by him to whom nothing has been intrusted. A position, if such an one could be found, which gave no opportunity for the exercise of manly qualities would stunt and dwarf our manhood. The Apostle in uttering his exhortation contemplated a sphere of action which is adapted to elicit manly qualities in the highest degree and afford them the largest possible scope for their operation.

In further unfolding the meaning of the text let us consider the style of manliness which it requires, and the scope for its manifestation under various particulars.

1. The Gospel approves and enjoins manliness in all the affairs of every-day life, even the most ordinary and trivial. The injunction of the text is valid in everything we do hour by hour and moment by moment. We should be under the sway of Christian principle as thoroughly when we are engaged in the most trifling and indifferent matters as when we address ourselves to those that are the gravest and most momentous. The spirit of the Gospel is an all-pervasive force; not intermittent, as though it bounded from mountain-peak to mountain-peak, touching only the summits of our lives, the loftier points which project above the ordinary level of our daily routine; but, like the atmosphere, it wraps the whole with a continuous and uniform pressure, resting on plain and valley as well as hill-top, enveloping alike with its gentle and insinuating touch every blade of grass and twig and grain of sand, and penetrating every tiny

nook and crevice with the same persistent energy as it holds in its embrace the vast globe of the earth itself.

We cannot sunder the little and the great in our lives, and, careless of the former, limit the realm of duty and of obligation to the latter. Our lives include a great multitude of little acts and scenes, each of which taken singly and by itself appears to be only of slight consequence, but which, viewed in the aggregate, assume great importance, since they are the constituent elements which make up the mass and determine the quality of the whole. Character is shown in these little things as the direction and force of the wind is shown by straws. We reveal what we are in our unguarded moments; and we do so all the more truly and distinctly that, when we are off our guard, our inmost disposition has unchecked sway. The man who even occasionally is mean, overbearing, slovenly, discourteous, or ungenerous in what he may account the veriest trifles must not be surprised if it is imputed to him and remembered against him as betraying a radical defect, which even conspicuous excellences cannot efface. The person who indulges his talent for mimicry or his fondness for a joke, even on trivial occasions, to the disregard of the feelings of a friend, or of honest and fair dealing, lays himself open to the inference that he is not dominated by the law of love and of truth.

Honor and uprightness can be shown even in sports. There is no excuse for ungentlemanly conduct anywhere. No one professing to be Christ's should be other than manly, generous, and noble at all times, and free from even the suspicion of what is mean, dishonorable, or unworthy of a true man. Discreditable behavior brings a reproach upon the Christian character and affixes a stigma to the Christian name which he has no right to place there. And it is all the more inexcusable, as the occasions are petty, that he should dishonor his Master and damage religion in the estimate of men for so slight a cause.

The Christian assuredly should not fall below men of the world in what is honorable and decorous, in all that ennobles and adorns character and life. Nay, he is bound to rise above them in these very respects, in which worldly men most pride and felicitate themselves. As the Christian has more exalted aims and higher motives and purer springs of action and heavenly aids, his whole life should be of a nobler mold, and more free from those deplorable petty weaknesses which so often stain lives otherwise excellent and destroy much of their power for good.

The Gospel spreads its hallowed influence over us every moment. The attraction of the cross, like the attraction of the sun, permeates all things alike, and holds atom and world in its noiseless yet powerful grasp. The great spiritual realities are ever real and should be ever operative. One grand motive, "for Christ's sake," should rule in every act and thought, and never for an instant be disregarded. We are bidden, whether we eat or drink or whatever we do, to do all to the glory of God. We are reminded that for every idle word we speak we must give account at the day of judgment. The Christian spirit should be infused into everything; Christian motives should govern everything; the law of the Christian life should give form to everything.

Not that we should make no distinction of time and place, or that we should act everywhere as if we were in church. The varied scenes of life are not to be met by one unvarying rigidity of demeanor. The Christian may unbend as well as other men. There is no reason why he should repress innocent mirth. He may have his seasons of recreation and of exuberant spirits. He need not be constantly oppressed by the sense of the awful and the infinite, much less perpetually wear a solemn-faced visage, as though it were a merit never to smile. But he can be pure and truthful and reverential and kind at all times. He can make the golden rule of Christ, which is the secret of the truest politeness and of gentlemanly conduct, his perpetual law. He can constantly have his heart full of the love of Christ, and of love to men, which shall dignify and sweeten his whole demeanor, which shall be the underlying stratum that supports and shapes the whole exterior surface of his life, and which without perpetually obtruding itself nevertheless crops out in all appropriate times and ways.

There is a divine and holy art in which some have made high attainments greatly to be envied, and which is worth pains and effort and circumspection to acquire, which adjusts the Christian character with dignity and grace to all the exigencies of our daily life, and without moping on the one hand or frivolity on the other maintains the purity and consistency of a Christian walk along with all that is engaging and sprightly and attractive in ordinary intercourse; which is ever filled with the spirit of Christ, and at the same time overflows with what is kindly and generous and sweet in human companionship; and which is a perpetual commendation of the Gospel by exhibiting the true style of manliness, which it is fitted to produce. This is what the Apostle enjoins upon us when in the common affairs of life he bids us, "quit you like men."

2. True manliness requires that a man should be a Christian. We respect manliness of character wherever shown, in earthly things and in the common intercourse of men. But we cannot refrain from saying to those who limit it to the concerns of this life, that their manliness is seriously defective and incomplete; that there is a disharmony in their life and conduct, one part standing in glaring contrast with the other and writing its condemnation. They recognize the propriety of the honorable and upright discharge of all that is incumbent in their human relations, but fail to meet the same when they are transferred to a higher sphere and far more sacred obligations are involved. They would spurn the thought of being insensible to favors received from earthly benefactors, and yet set at naught the abounding grace and love of their heavenly Friend. Priding themselves upon their punctilious integrity, they withhold from the Most High that which is his due. Nothing shocks them more than the unfilial behavior of a child, though themselves utterly undutiful to their Father in heaven. They regard with contempt the man who wastes his life on trifles, while yet they employ their

own immortal powers on things that perish with the using. The lesson of the text to such is that not only in-things seen and temporal, but also in those that are unseen and eternal, they should quit themselves like men.

3. The Apostle enjoins upon us manliness in the Christian life. In the exercise of grace, in the discharge of Christian duty, quit you like men. A due regard to our manhood not only requires that we should be Christians, but that we should be manly Christians; that we should not content ourselves with a merely nominal Christianity, or with a pusillanimous and ignoble Christianity, but that our spiritual faculties should be duly exercised and in full vigor, and that our spiritual life should be upon a plane worthy of the nature which God has given us. That we may the better comprehend what is thus demanded of us, let us briefly glance at some of those qualities which should characterize our religion.

(1) Manly strength and courage. There is a demand in the Christian life for the highest qualities of soul. There are tasks which must be performed with energy and perseverance. There are foes that must be met with unshrinking intrepidity and stout resistance. There are hardships which must be borne with patience and unmurmuring

fortitude. Soft effeminacy or childish weakness and timidity will not answer in the Christian ranks. By the cross to the crown, through suffering to glory, is the path that was trodden by Jesus and to which he summons us. Native strength is here inadequate. It is perfect weakness. We need the strength which God alone supplies. "He giveth power to the faint; and to them that have no might he increaseth strength." The stripling David can in his name encounter his giant adversary. Babes in Christ, as was fabled of the infant Hercules, strangle the old serpent. It is required of them that they be strong in faith, with a firm grasp upon the promises, doing all things, daring all things, enduring all things for Christ's sake. There is no room for cowardice and vacillation and unmanly shrinking from what is difficult and toilsome. Christ must be followed through evil and through good report; his commands must be obeyed at all hazards; the burdens which he lays upon you must be borne without faint-heartedness. Quit you like men.

(2) Men are possessed of reason. The text therefore enjoins it upon you to act as rational beings, with intelligence to comprehend the situation in which you are and the matters in reference to which you are called to act; to put a proper esti-

mate upon the ends to be pursued, and to know how to use the means requisite for attaining them. When men are engaged in great enterprises or momentous interests are involved, they bestow upon them earnest thought, carefully considering each step that they take, that all may be done wisely and well. And how can they do differently when the issues at stake are the salvation of the soul and the glory of God? And especially when truth and duty are plainly set forth in the Word of God, so that he who has ears may hear, and he who has eyes can see, and he who has reason can understand, what is to be thought of him who deliberately stops his ears and shuts his eyes, preferring darkness to light? What of him who will not ponder the paths of his feet, nor make diligent use of the means of grace and of spiritual growth, thus remaining ignorant and unskillful and in the lowest stages of religious progress, instead of growing in knowledge and growing in grace, and learning how to make the most perfect use of his powers in the service of Christ? Here again you are bidden to act like men.

(3) Men are free agents, endowed with the power of choice, at liberty to choose their own course, to act in accordance with the motives that are present to their minds. He is in a pitiable case who in the

presence of the most powerful motives that should instantly decide his course is hesitating, irresolute, and unable to make up his mind; or who with strange fatuity chooses in opposition to the noblest and best impulses of his nature. If with the mighty motives of the Gospel before us we can remain undecided, or our wills are so enslaved by Satan and by sin that we choose the reverse of what we know we should, and what our highest interests demand, we act as idiots or maniacs, not as men. The Apostle would have us always and evermore be men.

(4) It is the distinguishing glory of men that they have a moral nature. They are capable of discerning right and wrong. They approve what is good; they condemn what is evil. Conscience is their supreme faculty. Duty and obligation rise above everything else. If you would fulfill the demand which your human nature lays upon you, do right. Learn your duty from the revealed will of God, and then do it, not of course in your own strength, which will not avail you, but by those divine aids which will surely be afforded those who humbly ask for them. Let there be no parleying with the enemy; no looking wistfully at what is forbidden; no yielding to temptation under the plea that it is only for this once, or under any plea

whatever. You can suffer the loss of a right hand or a right eye; you can take joyfully, if need be, the spoiling of your goods, or rejoice if you are counted worthy to suffer shame for Christ's glorious name; but settle it with yourself that you cannot surrender principle, you cannot offend against God.

(5) Consider once more the rank which man holds in the scale of being: the lord of this lower world; made in the image of God; his nature kindred to the divine nature; admitted to friendly intercourse with God; made capable of knowing, loving, adoring his Maker, and in a sense quite peculiar to himself of glorifying him; endowed with a self-conscious, immortal spirit, which is worth more than the whole vast frame of material nature, and which shall continue to live when the sun itself has gone out in darkness. Of what exalted dignity is man, and what a demand is thus laid upon you to act in a manner worthy of your noble nature, as befits your high parentage and the grand destiny that awaits you! Eschew, then, all that is low, groveling, and despicable. Aspire to what is more in accordance with your high rank. Set your affections on things above. The transitory, the unsubstantial, and the trifling do not deserve the chief place in the esteem of men, who were made for higher things.

(6) But the dignity of human nature stands on far loftier ground than this, and it makes a yet stronger appeal to us. The incarnation and the atonement tell, as we never could have imagined it otherwise, the value of the human soul in the eyes of our divine Redeemer. The love that was shown, the price that was paid, the whole array of means and instrumentalities that have been set in operation, the subordination of all providence and, as it would appear, of creation itself to this crowning achievement of the Godhead, the work of our salvation, with which the Most High has condescended to link the supreme and most effulgent manifestation of his own glory in each of the sacred Persons —all this, while it is adapted on the one hand to humble us in the dust that such unexampled grace should have been shown to us in our littleness and our unworthiness, on the other hand unspeakably exalts us. His gentleness has made us great. What honor is conferred upon us in making us the objects of such divine regard! What enlargement of soul, what changed conditions, what new capabilities result from the employment upon us of this almighty celestial agency! And what possibilities are opened before us of indefinite and unending progress in all that is pure and good and holy and great!

Man redeemed is lifted up to a loftier and more conspicuous plane than he occupied at his creation. Believers in Christ are born of a new celestial birth, sons of God, heirs of heaven, wedded to the only-begotten Son, and with the assurance given them that they shall sit with him upon his throne. What new emphasis is thus imparted to the injunction, "Quit you like men." Degrade not a nature on which God is putting such abundant honor. Learn from the life of Jesus how a citizen of heaven should behave himself on earth. That is our pattern of manhood. We shall be men according to the true Gospel conception, if in all things we follow him, and resolutely refuse to stoop to that which would have been impossible for him.

In these various senses, then, you are bidden to be men in the whole round of Christian duty; in all your works of piety and devotion, in the cultivation of grace in your hearts, and in the manifestation of it in your outward lives act up to the demands of your noble nature, exhibit manly strength and courage, make full use of your reason, your free will, your moral sense, remember the exalted rank accorded to man in the creation, and the still higher rank to which he has been lifted by redemption.

The time that has already elapsed admonishes me not to trespass longer upon your patience, but

I must crave your indulgence while in a single word I suggest the application of my text to your seminary life and to your life-work. We form a little community in this institution of a peculiar kind, with our relations to one another and to those outside, with our special occupations and engagements. Now in all this be men. Let there be no petty childishness, nothing ignoble, no unmanly inconsistencies, no procrastinations, no neglects, no duties half performed or slovenly done. Maintain a character worthy of yourselves, in all things small and great, whether in these halls or out of them.

And when in due season you shall enter upon the full work of the ministry, if in God's distinguishing grace you shall be intrusted with those high functions, the highest and most sacred ever committed to human hands, then quit you like men, with all that union of strength and tenderness and all those manly qualities which this implies. If ever men can be roused to the full employment of all their faculties by grandeur of position, and nobility of work, and the magnificent sphere of action that is opened before them; by the high authority with which they come charged and the auxiliaries that may be summoned to their aid; by the opportunities afforded; by the certainty of success; by the splendor of the rewards; by the loftiness of their aims—this is surely the case in the very highest degree with the ambassadors of God to men, who are commissioned in Christ's name to carry forward his work of blessing here below, elevating human character, lifting burdens off of heavy hearts, stimulating to pure and noble deeds, enriching men with heavenly wealth, dispensing freely of God's richest, costliest bounty, bringing new glory to God, assisting in their heavenward journey the heirs of salvation to whom angels delight to minister, and aiding in the recovery of this lost world to God and goodness. If there be any work known amongst men which should call into full exercise the highest qualities of mind and heart, which can never be suffered to degenerate into a matter of routine or perfunctory performance, but in which the whole man should be most thoroughly engaged, it is the work of the ministry of the Gospel. Quit you like men, and let it be your aim to lead every one who hears you, or whom you can influence, to manliness and manly deeds.

THE POWER OF CHRIST'S RES-URRECTION.

BY THE LATE PROF. CASPAR WISTAR HODGE, D.D., LL.D.

"*That I may know him, and the power of his resurrection.*"—PHILIPPIANS 3:10.

THE resurrection of our Lord is set in four distinct relations in the New Testament.

I. It came, from the first preaching of the Gospel, most prominently into view as the evidence of the truth of Christ's claim to be the Saviour of the world. As fulfilling prophecy, both of the Old Testament and of Christ himself, it brought evidence of the divine purpose of salvation. As the manifestation of divine power in a result so transcendent, it furnished the attestation of Christ's claim to be the sacrifice and the life of all who believe. And as the exhibition of the love of God, it added to the attestation of omnipotence the actual exhibition of that power as grace, triumphing over sin and death and working out the salvation of men to its completion in spite of the most dreaded obstacles. In this aspect of it the resurrection of the Lord became the corner-stone of the Church, the essential proof of all that he claimed to be and all that he promised to do for those who trusted him. And in this aspect also it was all-comprehensive, because the whole of what was necessary to be received of the teaching concerning Christ's person and his work was included in its proof. If Christ rose, he was true; and all he taught himself or by his apostles was true. If he was true, he was divine; the Atonement for sin, the Author of spiritual life, the Giver of eternal life to all who believed. So that by the conditions of its first promulgation the resurrection was the Gospel; belief in the resurrection was faith in Christ; and the proclamation of the good news of salvation was the preaching of Jesus and the resurrection. The conflict of the truth was with Pharisees, who denied the fact because they repelled the claims and disliked the character of Christ; with Sadducees, who scorned the doctrine itself, and denied Christ because of it; with philosophical objectors, who disputed its truth on the ground of the difficulties it presents to reason, or because the benefit which it promised seemed at best doubtful. And so the Gospel won its victory over unbelief in this doctrine, until it was enthroned in the very heart of the Church, and crowned in

Gospel, Epistle, and Apocalypse as the central truth of the New Testament. And the power of the resurrection does not wane. It stands to-day, amid all assaults of unbelief, the acropolis of our faith, founded on the rock of divine truth, with the power of God vital within it for the world's salvation and the light of heaven resting upon it, keeping securely all our hopes of immortality.

II. But the power of the resurrection is not alone in the testimony it gives, but is associated with the innermost life of Christians. "That I may *know* him, and the power of his resurrection, and the fellowship of his sufferings." It is not the knowledge of an historical fact addressed to the intelligence, but inward knowledge, such as is conveyed by the light of the Spirit of God and is experimentally apprehended and incorporated with the Christian life. To know Christ is not to know what is taught about him, nor what he did; it is to have the spiritual experience of his personal presence with the soul; and knowing Christ is here expressed under the particulars of knowing the power of his resurrection and the fellowship of his sufferings. That power, therefore, has its sphere of operation in the most vital processes of spiritual life, and the resurrection of Christ is thus set in the most intimate relations with Christian experience.

Thus the resurrection is intimately connected in the New Testament with justification by faith. In this context Paul is suddenly moved to warn his readers against those who taught them to trust in the law. He sketches his own eminent advantages under the law, but declares that he counts them all but "loss, that I may win Christ, and be found in him, not having mine own righteousness, which is of the law, but that which is through the faith of Christ, the righteousness which is of God by faith: that I may know him, and the power of his resurrection, being made conformable unto his death." Here is the righteousness of the law on one side, and on the other the righteousness of God by faith. What Paul desires is to be found in Christ—that is, to have that union with Christ which secures the possession of the righteousness which he gives, and which brings spiritual experience of the power of his resurrection. The resurrection is evidently closely allied with Paul's doctrine of justification by faith. Only they who have the righteousness of faith can know the power of the resurrection in this experimental sense; and the power of the resurrection is manifested in producing the assurance of justification. In Romans 4: 24, 25, this relation is even more clearly established, where Paul, in illustrating his doctrine by the case of Abraham, who believed that God could fulfill his promise of raising the living from the dead, says that his faith was imputed for righteousness, and not for his sake alone, but "for us also, to whom it shall be imputed, if we believe on him that raised up Jesus our Lord from the dead; who was delivered for our offenses, and was raised again for our justification." That is, he was delivered unto death as a propitiation for our sins, and was raised again for our justification; emphatically declaring that our justification is not complete without the resurrection of Christ. We are not, indeed, to understand that his resurrection stands in the same relation to our justification that his death sustains, nor that it forms a constituent part of the sacrifice for sin. It is not penalty, it is reward; it is not suffering, it is triumph; it is not humiliation, it is exaltation to glory; it is not death, but the victory over death. But no process of conflict is complete without the victory, no labor without its reward. On God's part, indeed, the righteousness is procured, accepted, and the pardon secured. But on man's part there is no completed justification without resurrection; and the resurrection of Christ is for justification.

1. This will appear when we consider that the resurrection was necessary to exhibit the nature of the death of Christ as an offering for sin,—

that he did not die as a sinner, nor as a man like other men holden under the power of death. There was evidence, indeed, in his life of absolute holiness; there was evidence in his miraculous power, in his heavenly teaching, in his character asserting its divine origin; but all this would receive an utter contradiction and denial if it were possible that he should continue under the power of death. The elements of sacrifice are : the sinner, needing expiation; the priest; the perfect offering; and God above all, who accepts and pardons and grants life as the reward. The justification is incomplete and inoperative if any of these parts be lacking. "The sting of death is sin, and the strength of sin is the law." And if Christ be not risen, there has been no victory over sin and no annulment of the law; and there can be no evidence for the sinner that the death of Jesus stands in any such relation to his faith as that the righteousness of God, which is by faith, is become his; or that, even though he died with Christ, he has a new and spiritual life in the soul. Paul traversed precisely this road in his religious experience. Jesus appeared to him as risen and glorified. Then he knew that his death had not been that of a malefactor or of a pestilent deceiver, but was the one offering for sin which was adequate, and that Jesus whom he persecuted was his Lord and Saviour. Peter testifies to the same effect, when he tells us, that from the despair and sadness of the disciples at the crucifixion, and the disappointment of their hopes that followed, they were "begotten again unto a lively hope by the resurrection of Jesus Christ from the dead." And the Jews, who could not receive the doctrine of a suffering Messiah, and to whom his ignominious death was an absolute bar to his claim, when they accepted Peter's testimony that he had risen again saw also in his death their atonement, and repented and were converted. We see the power of his resurrection for justification.

2. It will appear further when we reflect that only by the resurrection was the dignity of his person, and consequently the value of his death as a sacrifice, exhibited. "He was declared to be the Son of God with power, by the resurrection of the dead." According to the doctrine of the New Testament, the humiliation of the Son of God in taking our nature, in assuming the form of a servant, and subjecting himself even to the death of the cross, can only be known and proved to be a humiliation by contrast with the exaltation to the right hand of God which ensues. The deity associated with man that was subject to death must be manifested by securing the weakness of humanity from the power of death. And the

human nature, suffering and brought low, must itself also share in the vindication, and become partaker in the heavenly glory. The exaltation of Christ reflects its glory upon his humiliation. The exaltation alone exhibits him to our faith and reverence in the character he claims as our Saviour. And when we see him who proves his origin by his present power and glory submitting to death, we then may estimate the value and significance of his death. Pain patiently borne, dignity asserting itself amidst brutal usage, calm self-surrender to a noble purpose, supreme love for men, even for enemies—these have their power. But we have seen them often and illustriously, thank God, in the annals of the race. But death of the Prince of Life; suffering in ineffable and spotless purity; patience in the Omnipotent One; the bosom of God from all eternity, and the throne and the praises of heaven to all eternity, set in contrast with the cross and with the sepulcher:—these give the power which it possesses to the death of Jesus. The dignity of his person alone exhibits the value of his death, and the power of his resurrection, therefore, is for our justification from sin.

3. And, as I have said, there is absolute necessity for the declaration on the part of God of the acceptance of the sacrifice. What assurance has the

sinner of forgiveness until God himself declares that he has forgiven? Vague trust in divine forbearance will not satisfy in such a case. We must know from himself what God will do. And the frown of God rested in darkness on the cross and on the tomb of Jesus until the dawn of the resurrection morning. Not till then was our justification assured.

4. And we are taught that he has ascended to the right hand of God, where he ever lives, and that his perpetual living before God is in order to his making prevalent intercession for us. We were justified in his death; we were justified in the pardon of God, spoken in peace to the soul; we are justified by faith. But we do not conceive of this justification as simply a transient act, done once and for all. It is a permanent relation between the forgiven soul and God, by which we ever live forgiven and secure upon the ever-living righteousness of Christ, and continue to live as pardoned sinners in the enjoyment of the fruits of his perpetual intercession. He was raised again for our justification. Could we conceive for a moment of an arrest in the divine purpose between the crucifixion and the resurrection—that the tomb of Jesus still guarded his mortal remains, that no angels announced his rising to the women, no disciples witnessed it to the

Church—and with all the teaching and the death of Christ what would be the heritage? Where would have been the Church founded on the faith of the dispirited and disappointed disciples; where our assurances of the life of God in the soul? What would be to us the graves of our dead? We might turn to the miserable caricatures of rationalism to write for us the history of the life of Christ and of the origin of the Church. And of the Church, and of heaven itself, we would utter the lamentation, instead of at the deserted grave: "They have taken away our Lord," and, leaving us only a shrine to visit in a holy sepulcher, his life and his Spirit are gone from us forever.

III. But if the power of his resurrection be for our justification, it is much more constantly in the New Testament, and more obviously, the source of the spiritual life of faith and of obedience. No form of statement is more familiar in St. Paul than this: "If ye died with Christ, ye also live in his rising again." In this familiar argument it is evident that we have something more than an appeal to gratitude or love to awaken the soul to effort to please him who has done so much for us. What incentive, indeed, so powerful could be found? But alas for us if there were nothing but our gratitude and love to depend upon as the forces of the Christian life! Nor is the conception of St. Paul that Christ has by his resurrection infused his own personal life into the Church, so that by faith his thoughts and energies become active in the free obedience of his people. For this it would seem that incarnation would be adequate without need either of death or of resurrection. But the doctrine is that the same Spirit of God that dwelt and dwells in Christ, making him in his humanity the organ of the divine Person, enabling him for his work and reviving him from death, dwells in the hearts of all those who believe in him. The same one, personal, all-powerful, and holy Spirit which is in him is the ascension gift to his Church. So that, having one Spirit, his people have one mind, one purpose, one life, as well as one destiny with him. This was the meaning of Christ when he told his disciples that his departure from them was in order to his sending the Holy Spirit. This was the intention of his words when he promised that he would be with them always, even to the end of the world.

1. And from this point of view we see clearly what Paul teaches the Ephesians, that in the resurrection of Christ we have a visible exhibition of the same energy which works in the hearts of all believers in their spiritual life; and therefore that we have the surest support to our faith that we

shall conquer in the conflict with sin, in the resurrection of Christ. "That ye may know what is the exceeding greatness of God's power to us-ward who believe, according to the working of his mighty power, which he wrought in Christ when he raised him from the dead, and set him at his own right hand in the heavenly places." The words express two things: first, that the power is the same, i.e., by the Holy Spirit; and second, that it is not only the pledge of the bodily resurrection of believers, but the pledge and cause of their spiritual resurrection. The same power working to the same end, and working, therefore, unto certain accomplishment. The omnipotence of God in the resurrection of Christ stands related, therefore, not only to the evidences of his truth, but it repeats the miracle in the spiritual experience of believers, who are raised by him to newness of life.

2. But this energy is more than pledged and more than illustrated in the resurrection. The language of the Apostle proves that it is actually imparted to the believer, conveyed in and by the resurrection of Christ. Read that wonderful argument in the sixth chapter of Romans: "Therefore we are buried with him by baptism into death: that like as Christ was raised up from the dead by the glory of the Father, even so we also should

walk in newness of life. . . . In that he died, he died unto sin once: but in that he liveth, he liveth unto God. Likewise reckon ye also yourselves to be dead indeed unto sin, but alive unto God through Jesus Christ our Lord." The argument of the passage is from the nature of union with Christ; if that be real and vital in his death, so that we are justified, then by the very nature and condition of that relation the union continues in his rising and in his present life. So that the Apostle teaches that there not only may be and should be, but that there was, the actual energizing of the soul of the believer with the power of God, in the resurrection of Christ. Read the same truth in Ephesians 2:5: "Even when we were dead in sins, God hath quickened" (rather did quicken) "us together with Christ, (by grace ye are saved;) and hath raised us up together, and made us sit together in heavenly places in Christ Jesus"—i.e., when he raised Christ he imparted life to believers. Such is this union with him that his resurrection is a related event, and they have spiritual life in him. And in his ascension and exaltation they are brought up spiritually from the power of darkness, and from life in sin, and made to be with Christ. Exaltation of the present life of faith as well as the future life of vision are alike included. And so when he argues in Colossians 2:12, 13, against an ascetic ceremonialism, his objection is that it dishonors that principle of life which we obtained from Christ when God raised him from the dead. In him ye have a spiritual circumcision and a spiritual resurrection, through the faith of the operation of God, who hath raised him from the dead. Faith in Christ and in the power of God which raised Christ are essentially the same thing and have the same life-giving energy.

3. Paul shows the power of the resurrection of Christ to sanctify, in the relation in which he sets the doctrine to the honor it gives to our mortal bodies. These frail, suffering, inadequate, sinning, treacherous, dying bodies are not despised under the Gospel, but kept as the temple of God and for the uses of the eternal life. Read the sixth chapter of 1 Corinthians, and what more profound statement of principles can be framed: "The body for the Lord, and the Lord for the body." It is not alliteration nor antithesis, "*The Lord for the body.*" "And God hath both raised up the Lord, and will also raise up us by his own power. Know ye not that your bodies are the members of Christ? . . . He that is joined unto the Lord is one spirit. . . . Know ye not that your body is the temple of the Holy Ghost which is in you, which ye have of God,

and ye are not your own?" The power of the resurrection is for the safeguard and the sanctification of these mortal bodies.

4. And the context sets this power of the resurrection for sanctification in yet another aspect, in its enabling us to endure the sufferings which are laid upon us in this life. Paul is speaking of his sufferings and self-denials, endured for Christ's Gospel, and he says that he counts them as the merest refuse of the feast if he can win Christ and know the power of his resurrection, and the fellowship of his sufferings, being made conformable unto his death. He alludes here, not to union by faith with the death and sufferings of Christ, but to the making up that which is lacking of the suffering of Christ for his body's sake, which is the Church. And in all active labor and personal self-denial which is to be endured in the great work, the power of his resurrection sustains and energizes and consecrates. Human life is become all sacred through this power; human nature glorified, because Christ was a man; the body honored because of the resurrection; suffering consecrated, death vanquished, the soul made pure and loving, the grave a peaceful and holy resting-place—all by means of the working of this holy life, which is in all who believe.

IV. Paul teaches that the resurrection of Christ is for our consolation. Under the conditions of its application you know how he dwells upon the truth as the assurance of our personal immortality, and as the invincible proof and absolute guarantee of our own bodily resurrection and triumph over death. "If we believe that Jesus rose, then also them that sleep in Jesus will God bring with him." "If the Spirit of him that raised up Jesus from the dead dwell in you, he that raised up Christ from the dead shall also quicken your mortal bodies by his Spirit which dwelleth in you." And this resurrection he teaches is to the eternal union with and vision of the Lord, and to the participation in his glory. "For when Christ, who is our life, shall appear, then shall we also appear with him in glory." The power of the resurrection, then, as we have seen, is for testimony to the truth, for justification by faith, for sanctification of life, and unto the life everlasting.

Briefly, three thoughts suggest themselves in consequence of this study of the truth:

1. How deep is our need of faith to realize the unseen in order to obtain the benefits of this doctrine. In the struggles and cares and vexations, and especially in the sins of life, how hard it is to *know*, inwardly and experimentally, the working of

this life of resurrection. And death! Ah! as we go along in life we become no better reconciled to the thought. Indeed, to the high-hearted enthusiasms of youth it may even be less terrible than to the sober understanding of experience. We become familiar, less sensitive, hardened by use. But it remains the same bitter, ruthless enemy to the end, wrenching from us our joy, and us from the light of life. Oh, for Paul's faith!— to "know Christ and the power of his resurrection, that we might count all things but loss for the excellency of the knowledge of Christ Jesus my Lord."

2. How wonderful is the unity of truth in its New Testament presentation. We may analyze and separate into its parts and establish associations in our minds with this or that doctrine of the Gospel; but in the words of inspiration itself we cannot touch the truth at any point without being led directly into relations with its most fundamental principle, and through every varying and rich abundance of association with all other truth and duty. All centers in Christ.

3. And hence how impossible it is to hope for the advantage of any part of this scheme as a part dissociated from the whole; to look for the manifestation of this spiritual life in blessing, if we do not

seek it in duty; to look for it in moral growth, unless we have it in justification and forgiveness; to have any hope in the resurrection of the dead, if we have not the present spiritual life of holiness; or to indulge any hope at all in this life or in the next, unless we be in Christ and know him.

DRIFTING.

BY THE LATE PROF. CHARLES A. AIKEN, PH.D., D.D.

"Therefore we ought to give the more earnest heed to the things which we have heard ["that were heard," R. V.], lest at any time we should let them slip ["lest haply we drift away from them," R. V.]."—HEBREWS 2:1.

WHAT is easier than slipping, or letting things slip? We need not do anything to slip. On the edge of a stair, on an icy path, on a fruit-skin that has been carelessly thrown upon the pavement, on the polished floor of a room in which we spend half our time, we may slip and become cripples for life, if we live to be cripples. Or if it is not we that slip, a bit of food slipping may strangle us; a sharp knife slipping may cut an artery; a valued possession slipping may be lost to us; a priceless opportunity for doing or getting good may pass away beyond recovery.

What one of the great movements of our life is in itself less noticeable than drifting? Its sources are far away out of our sight, in arctic or southern seas, in tidal movements, in convolutions of the coast, in irregularities of the ocean's bed, in storms that have been raging in other latitudes and longitudes than ours. The movement and pressure of the currents is quiet and noiseless. Things about us move with us, and we take less notice when all things pass on together. A cyclone so arouses and excites us as in extreme cases to paralyze us, and to take away the little power we had before the bursting of the storm. Drifting, we are lulled into a false security, and find, it may be, that at the last we cannot help ourselves in the false or perilous position into which we have—only drifted. On how many sandy beaches and rocky shores do hulks of goodly ships and bones of gallant men tell of the danger that is hidden in drifting! And when at the great day the sea shall give up its dead, who can count the hosts that shall come up out of its depths, because unsuspected currents bore them to the spot that was to be their tomb! The seamen may have been watching clouds, winds, the barometer, the compass—all but their charts; or, if their charts also, these were the work of half-instructed and finite men that could not know and record everything.

So in the social, political, intellectual, moral, and spiritual life of men drifting is one of the most constant and prolific causes of disaster. We might fill our hour with instructive and impressive illustrations from biography and history. Nor need we be learned in these departments of literature before we can find apt and effective enforcement for this lesson from the record-book of human life. The memory of a child can recall many unfortunate or evil conditions and experiences into which he never went purposely, but was carried along unawares, giving himself up to the forces that moved him. There is no hour of the life of the oldest of us that has not felt the power of these currents. Well for us if we have taken timely and sufficient warning, and so escaped the jeopardy in which we were.

This aspect of human life is very distinctly brought before us in our text, and furnishes our simple and practical theme—*drifting*.

Some of the considerations that I shall urge bear with equal propriety and force upon the life of all; others find their full application only in the case of Christian men and the Christian life. There is need enough that men be put on their guard in respect to social, financial, political, intellectual drifting; our great present concern is with the moral and spiritual life.

There is a drifting which tells of disaster already experienced, while it renders further disaster more probable. If her rudder-chains have given way, the powerful engines of the "Majestic" herself cannot keep her out of the trough of the sea or away from the ledges that line the coast. With a strong gale driving a vessel upon a lee shore, if her anchors find no holding ground she will soon be among the breakers. So in life there is a drift that lies midway between evil in the past and evil to come. Disabling calamity or overmastering vices may have made a man an easy and helpless prey to any strong current of influence that lays hold upon him. The lesson and caution of our text relate to a different class of phenomena—where power is not impaired or gone, but only not in use.

If we seek first for answers to the simple questions when, why, how we drift in so many things, in so many ways, even in the religious life, we shall better judge of the unworthiness and peril of it, and shall search more eagerly for a way of escape. Conscience will be aroused and give new emphasis to our text, as it teaches us that "*we ought to give the more earnest heed to the things that were heard, lest haply we drift away from them.*" We shall feel the force of the "*therefore*" with which the text begins.

Drifting always gives token of power at work. The force that is acting may be diffused and not concentrated; it is none the less force. It will be less noticeable if acting over a wide area; its pressure may at any given moment, at any given point, be more gently exercised; it may yet effect very substantial and serious results. A sudden blast coming upon us unnoticed might beat down or overturn the boat in which we were floating a moment before without apprehension. A few weeks ago I saw a miniature cyclone whirl rapidly over a small sail-boat that came directly into its path. The two occupants, seeing its approach, had, quick as thought, lowered their sail, dropped their anchor, thrown themselves down in the bottom of the boat, and were safe. Unobservant, one may drift very agreeably, under a gentle pressure, upon shoals or among reefs, and if wreck is escaped it may be a long and weary way back to the course on which he would be moving. It did not seem to be power that was carrying him out of the way; if it could be concentrated and measured, it might be found sufficient to sweep away massive barriers. Or it may be some hidden undercurrent that has taken us into its grasp. Of such the ocean must be full to keep the seas within the bounds appointed for them. In shallow waters, not showing themselves upon the surface, they may lay hold upon the vessel's keel and carry us whithersoever this unsuspected governor listeth. There are many such undercurrents in life, more dangerous because hidden. So long as nothing upon the surface attracts attention and awakens us to vigilance and effort, we are too ready to presume upon our safety and remit our activity. No summer passes that does not bring from popular seaside resorts a gloomy list of deaths by drowning, due to the fact that unobservant and over-confident swimmers had fallen inadvertently into the grasp of a treacherous current that was too strong for them and gave its warning too late.

The social and individual life of man is full of currents and their effects. The movement of our life is not all toward chosen ends. It is not wholly under the dominion of clear present intelligence, and high and worthy principle and purpose. What we do, what occurs with us, is not always decided by our own deliberate and justifiable judgment, or indeed by any other specific and recognizable choice.

Personal habit is one of these currents. Our habits, even in the highest and most important concerns, are often formed, and become very persistent and controlling, without much warrant for satisfaction on our part in and with them. Good habit is a mighty power in aid of a worthy life when ends are wisely chosen and energies trained to work easily and almost automatically. But many of our habits in every department of our life do not in any worthy way come into being, and into the place of control which they have gained for themselves. We do and continue to do until the doing becomes almost a second nature. Only under special inducement, and only with strenuous endeavor, do we act otherwise. And it might cause embarrassment and shame were we called to justify or apologize for our habit. Such acts and courses of action do not so much as attract our own attention, however it may be with the attention of others; they no longer summon us to deliberation; we have left behind in their case that serious discriminating criticism to which we may still subject distinct and new activities. How much of our life drifts in currents of individual habit!

General social usage is another current. Here it is not our own past action that has determined the kind of force or the direction of the movement that is bearing us along. It is the choice or habit of others, or some power more complex yet, by which we are encompassed and mastered and carried on, with very little consent or thought, perhaps without suspicion. We have passed neither intellectual nor moral judgment upon it. The pinch of conscience is felt the less, because it is what others are and do that so largely decides our doing; and our conscience readily excuses itself from presuming to judge them.

Where we are all moving together it is so easy to take little account of the direction of the movement, or even of the fact that we are in motion. We are not drifting through or away from our environment, but with it; and we may need to look at some distant landmark to see in what course we are all going together. We shrink from being accounted odd or out of sympathy with our constant and necessary companions. We are unwilling to be thought censors of our friends.

Sometimes these social usages are of very large dimensions, covering wide spaces and long periods. Many influences have conspired to make them what they are. Their springs lie hidden in part in a distant past. We may be contributing our little quota of support to them now, but they were before us, and will be after us; we found them, we leave them behind; but for the time being we are in many ways and at many points subject to their pressure. It often becomes a delicate and difficult moral problem what our responsibility is in regard to them, not so much with respect to their existence, as with reference to our attitude toward them. Too often we raise no question; we only drift with them. Within this large and general social movement there will always be found in every particular society or community forces at work creating a local drift, which may be quite distinct from or independent of the greater currents that bear men along. Contrasts become more marked, are more quickly noted, and will be more sharply criticised when one deviates from the custom of those close about him, and seems by his action to reflect upon the propriety of theirs. Therefore in the interest of peace and of good-fellowship one sometimes falls in with that which his immediate fellows do which he does not approve.

Even in limited and select communities (like our own) where conditions might be supposed to be at their best, where mental and moral faculties should be most cultivated and alert, where the sense of personal responsibility should be most highly developed and strongest, where men should most surely know what they do and why they do it, traditional usage, or temporary and local currents of some other sort, may suspend that searching scrutiny and that clear and well-defined individual decision which are so essential to high and right action. Our very sense of security in our favorable conditions may lead us to go unquestioning with the multitude. Our hand drops the helm and we drift. We quietly divest ourselves of responsibility, and do what others do, and because they do it, instead of being vigilant and active in moral decision. We fall into the state of the people whom our Lord reproved with the question, "Why even of yourselves judge ye not what is right?" We forget that we cannot so transfer responsibility to our neighbors or our circumstances, even the best, or sink ourselves in the mass to which we for the time belong.

These illustrations will sufficiently prove that there is a great deal of drift in this life of ours, omnipresent, incessant, and often of grave import, and show some of its sources and something of its nature. We are now ready to appreciate and estimate the unworthiness and the perils connected with such surrender of ourselves to the currents that may be sweeping about us and pressing upon us.

1. This drifting *dishonors and imperils manhood*, especially its highest type, Christian manhood. In it we resign some of our highest dignities as men; we sacrifice some of our most precious privileges; we throw away without consideration or equivalent some of the most essential safeguards of our welfare; we repudiate responsibility.

There is a spirit of the age very real and influential; we as men cannot be wholly independent of it, yet we need not be, nor can we properly be, in unquestioning subjection to it. As social beings we must feel in a thousand ways the influence of the usages, movements, tendencies of the larger or smaller society in which we sometimes seem to be such insignificant units; but as men we are not the creatures, the vassals of these forces. In many things and in many ways we are moved involuntarily by others; we tend to move with others.

It is not true of all the currents in this social life which we live among our fellow-men that they are evil or tend to evil. It is often of the greatest advantage to us that we may have the benefit of very much in the social condition, and in the direction and volume of the movement of society, that we could never have produced, but of which we may avail ourselves to our great profit. But when we most congratulate ourselves on the prevalence of truth and right in the social order or movement of our age, or land, or particular community, it would be a poor tribute to pay the human sources, much more the divine Author of our advantages, if we on their account consent to be the less men. One need not be a man to drift; a log, a dead weed can do that, and violate no law of its being and forfeit no preëminence. And surely it is most unworthy of a man, and most perilous to manhood, to be borne this way and that, without attempt at control; without knowing or asking why and how and whither; and most of all in those spheres of life where manly endowments are of highest worth and responsibility presses most heavily.

We need not all aspire to be heroes in any distinctive way; yet there are heroic possibilities in all true manliness, and nothing is in stronger contrast with the heroic in character and action than habitual inadvertence, and the surrender of ourselves to the mastery of the currents that may chance to be prevailing about us. Quitting us like men, we shall at least not drift. The heroic stems strong currents and forces its way against them. It faces and withstands multitudes, instead of seeking them as its company and waiting for their suffrage or their practice as its criterion of truth and right; it can stand alone in its witness and its work; it is self-sacrificing rather than self-indulgent and compliant. The hero cannot be named who drifted to his noble service and its renown.

2. Drifting *puts in jeopardy all the important interests that are committed to our charge.*

As part of the plan of our life, drifting may be allowable as the occasional recreation of an hour on a summer holiday, when we thoroughly know our situation, and only seem to abandon all concern for the course and movement of our craft, ourselves, and our agreeable companions. Even then he would be worse than foolish who should resign himself to forces and conditions of which he knew nothing, and with which it was not in his power at any moment to deal intelligently and resume the dominion that he had never really renounced. But in the more serious relations of life, in which there is no holiday putting us off duty, suspending the responsibilities and the issues connected with our many momentous trusts, it is much more impossible that we divide accountability with—we know not what. Unless we proclaim ourselves utter fools we cannot assume that the currents to which we resign ourselves will care for us and our concerns (they are *ours*) as well as or better than we ourselves. If it is not true that all currents in life are evil or tend to evil, neither may we presume that all are good or tend to good. Be they ever so good, they are not charged with our affairs, nor may we form a partnership with them, sharing risks and profits. The conduct of the business of our life belongs under God to us.

Alert and in the exercise of all our powers we are weak enough, and have difficulties and oppositions enough to overcome. And faithfulness is faith in what? In the currents about us? So far as we are fully engaged in and faithful to that which is committed to our charge, and him who has committed it to us, we may trust, under divine guidance, to be brought in due time to our desired haven. But winds and seas will not bring us there of themselves. A south wind blowing softly may give place to Euroaquilo, and we be "driven to and fro in the sea of Adria," escaping like Paul and his fellow-voyagers with but our lives. Gentle currents may lead on to plunging waters, seeking exit this way and that, among the ledges that would block their course. In a good boat, with four sturdy pilots at the wheel, one may pass, as thousands do every summer, with nothing more than a pleasurable excitement, over the rapids at Lachine, and smile at the black rocks and the boiling waters that surround him. Drifting over that same course there would be little chance that those rocks (on which one's epitaph could never be written) would prove anything less than perpetual uninscribed monuments to the folly which would surrender itself to the currents that but a little way above flowed so smoothly.

Drifting will not accomplish for us any part of the appointed work of life; will not build up holy character; will not correct distortions or supply deficiencies; will not enrich us with treasures of knowledge and wisdom; will not stamp upon us the image of Christ; will not fulfill any duty of ours to other souls. The world, society, will not be the better for our drifting through it or in it. The salt parts with something of its former saltness. Losing something constantly, as we drift, of the possible vigor and quality of our former character, how shall we tone up other's characters? How shall we help others to profounder reverence for truth or more controlling respect for principle while we are dismissing truth and principle from their ascendency over ourselves? Our gains as we fall in with the current are wholly illusory; our sacrifices are real and serious, and may easily become irreparable.

3. A graver aspect yet of such a life is *its disloyalty to God, and the peculiar dishonor which it puts upon Christ.* These are the points specially emphasized in our text.

God has not so fashioned us, and so endowed us, and so watched over us, and so had pity on us and paid the costly price of our redemption, that we might give ourselves over to inadvertence and inactivity. We cannot overestimate his rights of control, and the reality of his efficiency in the world of nature and of men. But we may misjudge the nature of his working, as we surely do if we take all the currents that are stirring among men as exponents of his will, and fancy that we most submit ourselves to him when we most completely resign ourselves to them.

We are to deal personally with him, and not in masses. "Acquaint now thyself with him, that it may be well with thee." His communications address themselves to our intelligence and sensibility and conscience and will, and summon them to their highest exercise. However many may with us be subject to his law, it is not our doing what others about us, few or many, may be doing that proves intelligent loyalty to him. If his providence over us is particular and his discipline of us individual, and the call of his Spirit and his enlistment of us in his service contemplate our gifts and opportunities, then nothing less personal and resolute and exclusive than the question, hourly renewed, "Lord, what wilt thou have me to do?" at all meets the conditions of the case. The asking must be ours, and the interpretation of the coming answer ours, and the decision ours, and the discharge of duty ours. We cannot drift on any current into true obedience to the will of God. And so to deal with him is to deny him. To float on the stream is neither to remember nor to surrender to his personal demands upon ourselves. It substitutes another rule and method of living.

All the connections of our text in the chapters that precede and follow remind us that God's chief and final communications to men are those made by his Son, and his chief requirements those made in behalf of his Son. His nature, his position and relations, his appointed offices and work, exalt him above all, whether men or angels, prophets or ministering spirits, to whom God had given other commission. He who demands of angels (all the angels of God) worship of the Son does not ask less of men. If we respond by giving up the control of our life, even in part, to any chance influence that may be stirring about us, it is not manhood only that we lightly esteem, it is not our own interests simply that we treat most indifferently and heedlessly imperil. Our disloyalty concentrates itself upon him who has been made the rightful Lord of our life, to whom it should all pay tribute. It is the testimony of Jesus of which the Scriptures are full. A life ruled by regard for that which is for the present easy and agreeable is strange dealing with the exalted Son, a strange requital of what he has done for us.

If all this be so, we cannot put too strong an emphasis on the affirmation of our text: "Therefore we ought to give the more earnest heed to the things that were heard."

Here is the affirmation of a dangerous possibility: we may drift away from the things that were heard when God spake in heaven and from heaven. If we do, where are we?

Here is the assertion of a strong obligation: we ought to give heed, to give heed more abundantly. It is not a mere intimation of propriety or a suggestion of expediency, it is a necessity that is announced. No fugitive seriousness of thought and solicitude, no pondering for a moment, no glancing at the situation, no mild pang of regret over our error and folly and sin, will be fair dealing with the case or will save us. Earnest heed is a necessity; "*we must.*" And earnest heedfulness is not enough; it must be rightly directed, and concentrated upon the things that most demand remembrance and the treatment to which they are entitled. No word of God may be lightly dealt with, and then put aside as having no more value for us. But there are words of his spoken of old to and of the Son that should rivet memory and thought, of which we should never lose sight. Drifting away from them is, above all other drifting, monstrous, impious, ruinous—monstrous dealing with truth and fact; impious treatment of him who spake, and of him of whom he spake; ruinous dealing with our own well-being. It was then and there, when the Most High so uttered his voice, that our duty was most clearly and unmistakably made known; then and there that the Saviour and his salvation were announced and offered; then and there that we learned who and what is our God, and who and what the Son of God, in his essential glory, his original and his conferred and acquired rights, his claims upon the allegiance of men.

Here is the choice that is offered us: subjection to Jesus Christ, and experience of his power to guide and save; and, on the other hand, drifting, to be guided and blessed and saved—by whom or what? Yet so inconsiderate are we, so ready to take our ease, so fond of floating on the current of the hour, so unmindful of our interest, so insensible to our true honor, so little impressed with our accountability, so little loyal to God, so unstable in our devotion to Christ, that even here we drift away, and because it is only drifting hardly notice it.

The *therefore* of our text should bring us to ourselves; that should rebuke and shame our inadvertence, our easy deference to custom, our weak compliance with what is common, popular, current about us, our giving account so little to God or to ourselves of what we are or do. In the presence of him who spake from heaven no heed will be felt to be untimely or excessive, no reverence too profound, no homage too adoring, no trust too absolute, no obedience too careful and scrupulous, no consecration too entire and comprehensive. Abiding in the presence of these mighty and glorious truths, we may hope, through the greatness of God's grace, to be carried on the full tide of their power into the presence of the King, to the rest that remaineth.

HOW WE SPEND OUR YEARS.*

BY PROF. WILLIAM M. PAXTON, D.D., LL.D.

"We spend our years as a tale that is told."—PSALMS 90 : 9.

THE year eighteen hundred and ninety-one has gone. Its times and incidents, once present, are now fast receding from our view, as if borne upon an ebbing tide, never to return. As we look backward, past joys sparkle like white-caps in the distance, and then vanish; past sorrows rise and swell in dark-blue waves, and diminish as they recede. The year has rolled out its last wave of privilege and opportunity, and disappeared forever. Nothing now remains but to bid it a last reflective farewell. As an appropriate farewell reflection, I propose the sentiment of the text: *"We spend our years as a tale that is told."*

What renders the parting affecting is that they are *our* years. "We spend," says the psalmist, "our years." Oh, it is sad and solemn to part with anything that is ours ! Whatever is so related to us as to be designated by this language of self-

---

* Preached on the opening Sabbath of the year 1892.

appropriation is dear to our hearts. *Our* father, *our* mother, *our* home, *our* church, are expressions of the dearest affinities of life. A day, if we can only call it ours—as, for example, the day of our birth—is more precious than all other days. We feel sad to bid it adieu and leave it forever. So with a year when it is linked to us by the same personal relation.

IN WHAT SENSE, THEN, WE INQUIRE, DOES THE PSALM-IST CALL THE FLEETING YEARS OF LIFE "OUR YEARS"?

There is not a single one of them that, strictly speaking, we can call our own. We have no right of proprietorship in them or authority over them. We can neither command, nor control, nor guide them. There is no Gibeon on which the hours pause at our bidding; no Ajalon where the night-watchers await our pleasure. Even Queen Elizabeth, with all the power and wealth of a kingdom at her control, could not command one inch of time.

And yet the years are ours; ours whether we will or not. They are linked to us as by a personal, responsible, and indissoluble relation. In the first place, THEY ARE OURS TO ENJOY.

Enjoyment is the appropriation by which a thing becomes truly our own. Without this there can be no real possession. A blind man may own one of Raphael's angels, but he cannot in the highest sense say, "It is mine." It is his by the law of property, but not by the law of nature; for as he cannot enjoy it, he is incapable of that appropriation which makes it truly his own. Just so the years are ours to enjoy. This was their primeval design. God made the years to be the measure of our joys; but sin perverts them to note the slow and weary transit of our woes. When God appointed the sun and the moon to "be for signs, and for seasons, and for days and years," it was to measure out the joys of Paradise. Each new day, and so each year, was a new gift of Heaven to enjoy. In this blessed sense the years are still our own. They come with "many a glorious throng of happy dreams." Each moment has its mercy, each hour its bursting hope, each day its "good and perfect gift," and each year its crown of loving-kindness. A year, therefore—nay, a day—unenjoyed is a robbery of self, a sin against Heaven. Better lose a jewel than a joy.

THEY ARE OURS TO EMPLOY.

Ours for the best and most valuable uses. They are our seed-time, to be employed in ploughing and sowing for the harvest of eternity. They are the woof and warp out of which we weave the web of life. They are a mine in which there is a mass of precious treasure, which may be dug for, and will be found if the labor is applied. They are a stream flowing swiftly by us, and when once past they are gone forever; but if seized as they come, and appropriated, they may be turned to the best of uses— to grind the grist of duty or irrigate the garden of the soul. Oh yes, the years are ours to use! They are the winds of time, and if we hoist our sails we may employ them to waft us to the shores of the heavenly Canaan.

But still more emphatically the Scriptures teach that the years are ours *as a working day.* Time is a little section cut out of eternity, and given us to do our work in. Hence the command, "Go work today in my vineyard!" There is no soul work beyond the grave. All that a poor sinner can do for his immortal soul must be done in that short span of time which intervenes between the cradle and the grave. But there is a still more important sense in which the passing years are ours.

THEY ARE OURS TO ACCOUNT FOR.

Time is a precious treasure given to us in trust as stewards, and we are responsible, not only for the principal, but for the interest. We have not only to account for each moment received, but for its use. We must return to God his own with usury. With every hour that God gives us he seems to say, "Take this and occupy till I come." A year past is therefore a year gone before to meet us at the Judgment. Every day is a charge against us in the book of life. Every moment that fills up the measure of our time comes to us like a messenger from another world, marks our conduct, and then hastens back with its report to the throne of God.

If, then, the years are ours by such a blessed, solemn, and momentous proprietary; if they are ours to enjoy, ours to employ, and ours to account for at the bar of God—*how do we spend them?* This inquiry, so deep and solemn in its import, is answered by the text,

"WE SPEND OUR YEARS AS A TALE THAT IS TOLD."

This answer not only expresses an inevitable fact, the rapid transit of life, but involves a censure. "We spend," literally, we consume, we waste our years, as if in listening to a tale that is told. Let us, then, dwell for a few moments upon the points of the comparison here presented.

WE SPEND OUR YEARS ILLUSIVELY—AS A TALE THAT IS TOLD.

The point of thought here is the correspondence between the false, unreal, fictitious way in which many spend their years, and the dreamy, excited illusions we experience in listening to a romantic tale. The comparison, you observe, is not to a sober history, but to an airy fiction. The allusion of the text is evidently to the legends, poems, and tragic romances which in the earlier ages of the world, especially in Oriental countries, were recited from house to house by traveling bards and minstrels. Those who listened to these engaging recitals— like those who now gaze upon a theatrical illusion —imbibed the spirit of the ideal scene, and were wrought into sympathy with the actors, till for the time being they lived and breathed under the spell of the enchantment, and then awoke to find it all an illusion.

Such, to vast multitudes, is life—a vain, unreal scene, a fictitious delusion, a succession of wanton hopes and bitter disappointments. They imbibe the spirit of the world; are wrought into sympathy with the passing pageant; hurry with feverish excitement from scene to scene and from act to act in the drama of life; and at its close awake to the realization that they have walked in a vain show, they have been the victims of a false and artificial excitement, they have wasted emotion in idle and foolish sympathies, and are now ending their years as a tale that is told.

Who, indeed, is there that to some extent has not experienced this illusion? Who has not found the magnificence of life's promise lost in the poverty of the accomplishment? Youth is fresh and bright with hopes never to be realized. Middle age is eager and sanguine, grasping after expectations which end in vacuity and disappointment. Old age, worn, sobered, wrinkled with care, and covered with the dust of toil, confesses that its days have been "few and evil." Industry digs for a hid treasure, which often disappears, like the fabled chest, as soon as the crowbar rings upon its iron lid. Ambition climbs for laurels that wither in its grasp. Pleasure, like a humming-bird, recedes from the silly child of sense as he approaches to seize it, and retiring from flower to flower, eludes his speed and cunning. Thus in a vain, unreal illusion "we spend our years as a tale that is told."

Is life, then, with its crowd of incidents and objects, an unreal phantasm? Is this great world, with its busy enterprise and potent energy, a dream, a pageant, a mere minstrel's tale? Nay, verily! The world, and life in the midst of such a world, is a reality. The illusion is not in life or in the world but in ourselves—in our own distorted vision, in our own deceitful and wicked hearts. The real becomes a fiction when viewed through a false medium, and even sober truth becomes falsehood when misconceived or falsely applied.

As a matter of experience, we all know that life is just what the mind and heart make it. The outer is but the exponent or expression of the inner life. The soul spreads its own hue over everything. To a fresh, genial spirit life is joyous and the world is clothed in a wedding-garment; whilst to the somber, melancholic mind all nature is shrouded in a funeral-pall. In the case of each the shroud and the bridal-robe are woven in the loom of their own feelings. "The universe," says another, "is the express image and direct counterpart of the souls that dwell in it. Be noble, and all nature replies, 'I am divine'; be mean, and all nature dwindles into contemptible smallness." To this we may add: be holy, and life is real and glorious; be sinful, and life perverted from its proper use is a gross delusion.

Solomon represents himself as having constructed a magnificent pile of every good thing under the sun, only to find it vanity in the end. What was the reason of Solomon's disappointment? He mistook the proper use and design of the good things of life, and thus, by his own perversion, they became an illusion. "Solomon," says a commentator, "would have found no disappointment in his houses if he had used them as houses; nor in his wealth if he had used it as wealth; but instead of this, he made them things to love and put his confidence in, and in that view all his successes were vanity and vexation of spirit."

Here, then, is the true solution of life's illusion. It is deceitful only as we use it deceitfully; it is false, because by perverting its end and uses we practice deception upon ourselves. Life properly understood and virtuously fulfilled is a scene of sublime reality, an arena of noble deeds, a discipline for the development of love, faith, and patience, and a school for exercise and evolution of immortal powers. Then let us break the spell of this false enchantment; for, believe me,

> "Life is real, life is earnest,
> And the grave is not its goal;
> 'Dust thou art, to dust returnest,'
> Was not spoken of the soul."

WE SPEND OUR LIVES AMUSIVELY, AS IF LISTENING TO A TALE THAT IS TOLD.

A tale is usually a momentary, trifling amusement. We listen, not for any serious or valuable purpose, but to be entertained or to pass away an idle hour. It is followed by no good or permanent results. The emotions, whether sportive or serious, terminate with the story, and both are speedily lost and forgotten. And in a manner similar to this are the years of life spent by no small part of the human race. The hearers of tales are not more perfectly the votaries of amusement during the period of rehearsal than are multitudes during the whole progress of life. In this way they waste, consume their years, as one who listens to a tale that is told. Many are active, energetic, industrious; but the great purpose at which they aim is enjoyment, without a wish exercised or an attempt made to become wise, virtuous, or useful. Mere butterflies, they flutter from field to field and from flower to flower, heedless that the summer in which they sport will be soon succeeded by a season of frost and death.

This may be true just as much of the active, energetic man of business, or of the stirring housewife, as of the mere child of passion and pleasure. They may pursue the enterprises and endure the toils of life for purposes merely amusive. The whole aim of all their plans and projects may be to say to their soul at some future day: "Soul, take thine ease; thou hast much goods laid up for many years; eat, drink, and be merry."

To such the successive stages of life bring no

solemn reflections. They consume one year and enter upon another, inquiring only, "how to-morrow shall be as to-day, only more abundant." Instead of learning, from past errors and past sins, future wisdom and reformation; instead of being admonished by reproofs, alarmed by judgments, solemnized and softened by affliction, and charmed to gratitude and repentance by the mercies of a gracious Providence, they hurry from enjoyment to enjoyment, and bustle from sport to sport, imbosomed and lost in the present gratification, forgetful that endless happiness must be gained, or endless misery suffered, in the world to come.

Now, against this mere amusive wasting of life the censure of the text is directed. Oh, how different is this manner of employing life from that to which it was destined by our Creator! By him it was intended to be to each one of us a day of probation and of grace, a season in which we were to renounce our sins, accept of the mercy offered to us through a Redeemer, and secure a title to a happy immortality. To turn it, then, from this grand object to purposes of mere amusement is one of the grossest of all perversions. It is to ignore the design of our Creator; it is to sink the soul into subserviency to the claims of the flesh, and it is to barter the birthright of our immortality for a mess of earth's pottage. If one of yonder stars should resign its glorious sphere and "sink to darkle in a rayless void," it would not be a greater perversion of the design of its creation than for an immortal soul, that might shine as an orb of light, to forego the distinctions of its spirituality, to burrow in the dust of worldliness, and pale its splendors amid the follies and lusts of an earthly carnalism.

If, then, the purpose of life is so important and life itself so solemn, how have you spent the past year? Have you consumed, wasted it for mere purposes of self-gratification, and are you now bringing it to a close amusively, as a mere tale that is told? The time is short, but to spend this shortness easily is arrant folly. He who wastes the life that now is sins against the life to come.

WE SPEND OUR YEARS SWIFTLY, AS A TALE THAT IS TOLD.

The former points of the comparison involved a censure, but this confronts us with a serious, solemn fact—the rapid transit of our years, the swiftness with which we pass from station to station in our hurried journey to the grave. "We spend our years as a tale that is told." Hours fly like words, weeks like sentences, months like chapters, and life like a tale quickly told.

> "The very breath which frames my words
> Accelerates my death."

"We die daily," says the Apostle; die as fast as time flies. We talk of dying, and die while we are talking. Existence here is a continuous death.

> "Our birth is nothing but our death begun,
> And cradles rock us nearer to the tomb."

Oh, what a fleeting, evanescent thing is life! "A vapor that appeareth for a little time, and then vanisheth away;" a wind that is present for a moment, and anon it is gone; a shadow that flits across the plain; a flower that blooms in the morning with a freshness and beauty that charms the eye, and in the evening it withers away; a journey from the cradle to the grave, rapid as the passage of the weaver's shuttle:

> "A fire whose flames through crackling stubble fly,
> A meteor shooting from the summer sky,
> A bowl adown the bending mountain rolled,
> A bubble breaking, and a fable told.
> A noontide shadow and a midnight dream."

These are emblems which aptly proclaim our earthly course.

Few who have passed the season of youth have failed to observe how imperceptibly we advance in years; how year after year is stealing on with a stealthy and even pace, and without our notice is bearing us into age and toward the darkness of the tomb. We grow old and approach our dying hour without being aware how rapidly we advance. The boy, the youth, the man, is looking forward to life, till suddenly he awakes from his dream and finds his life is chiefly spent. His years have sped away he knows not how, like a tale that is told.

Not only is the passage of our years rapid, but increasingly rapid as we advance in life. As the interest of a tale deepens the time passes more swiftly, until at length, absorbed in the crisis of the plot, hours flee apace, and we take no note of their passage. Just so in life. The flight of years grows swifter as we advance in age. As cares cluster and the drama deepens, hours, days, and years pass unnoticed, and men look back, worn and bewildered, wondering how it is. Time seems to run with breathless speed as we draw near the goal of death, as if it were eager to bear us to the grave. This fact none have failed to notice. The explanation is that *time*, correctly speaking, is nothing more than a succession of ideas. These ideas are less numerous and the impressions they make upon the mind less permanent in old age than in youth, and, consequently, "the road of declining life has fewer stones to mark our progress along it."

THE COMPARISON OF THE TEXT FURTHER INDICATES HOW SHORT OUR PAST LIFE APPEARS IN THE REVIEW.

If we take the standpoint of an aged man, and look back, his threescore and ten years seem compressed into the briefest compass. So much of the incident of life has faded from his memory, that it all seems like a tale that is told. "An old man," says another, "can live over all his years again at one sad sitting." "Childhood's happy thoughts, youth's painted phantoms, manhood's early struggles; the clutched prize, which proved a shadow; the dreaded ill which never came—what are they in the review but like the chapters of a well-wrought tale—only too natural in their telling!"

Hence the mournful review of Jacob in answer to Pharaoh: "The days of the years of my pilgrimage are a hundred and thirty years; few and evil have the days of the years of my life been." "*Few and evil.*" "For what," asks a writer, "were the living things of that history? The life of that long life? Oh, they were just the marked passages, the mere headings of chapters—his vision at Bethel, his service for Rachel, his wrestling with the Angel, his tidings of a long-lost son saving his gray hairs from being brought with sorrow to the grave. Much of the rest of that one hundred and thirty years was one great undotted blank—the unremembered parts of a now concluded tale."

The figure of the text includes another point of comparison.

YEARS PAST, LIKE A TALE THAT IS TOLD, ARE USEFUL ONLY FOR THEIR MORAL.

They are gone beyond the possibility of recall, and whatever advantages, or privileges, or opportunities they presented when they were present with us are now gone with them into the abyss of eternity. The past is, therefore, of no profit now, save as the food for solemn reflection.

Let us, however, as from a tale already told, endeavor to deduce the moral.

I. *To all of us it has been a year of prolonged life.*

We have enjoyed a whole year more of valuable time than we had any right at the beginning of it to assure ourselves of. The unfruitfulness of the former year might have justly subjected us to the sentence pronounced upon the barren fig-tree: "Cut it down, why cumbereth it the ground?" But the Saviour prayed, "Spare it yet another year," and our lives were continued, and riches of time given us to spend, more than we had any right to expect. The moral, then, obviously is the exceeding goodness and long-suffering of God, and the necessity of careful self-examination to see if we have done that which we were spared to do; if we have brought forth this year "fruit meet for the Master's use."

II. Again: *It has been to many of us a year of great spiritual opportunity and privilege.*

Let us go back and place ourselves, in thought, where we stood at the beginning of the year. What a wide door of privilege opened before us; what advantages for spiritual instruction and improvement; what opportunities for glorifying God and saving souls; what means for advancement in knowledge and growth in grace; what facilities for prayer, for holy meditation, for heavenly-mindedness, for self-examination and self-correction, for assuring ourselves of our interest in Christ and of our title to eternal life! Compute the sum of all these individual things, and consider, if effected, what spiritual enrichment you would now enjoy. Remember now that when the year began all this was possible, and what is the moral you deduce? Obviously a lesson of fervent gratitude to God for such a harvest season of privilege, and of deep humiliation for our failures to reap the benefits. A lesson of repentance for the past, and endeavors after new obedience for the future.

III. Again: *To most of us it has been a year of domestic and social enjoyment.*

Our boards have been covered with plenty, our homes have smiled with gladness, and domestic affections and family ties have endeared us to life. Let us, then, draw the moral thus: God has spared me another year to my family, and his goodness to me and mine place me under a new obligation to love and serve him. Let me, therefore, begin the new year by the more entire consecration of myself and my household; by the more faithful instruction of my children in the way of life; and with a full purpose of heart that "as for me and my house, we will serve the Lord."

Time would fail to particularize. The moral of the year differs according to the position and circumstances of each individual. To the bereaved and afflicted it is a lesson of humble resignation and faith; to the tempted, an admonition to cling closer to him who was "tempted in all points like as we are, yet without sin"; to the unconverted it is a call to repentance before the door is shut; to the young, a warning that another year has passed, and that the invitation grows more urgent—"Son, give me thine heart." To one and all it is a lesson of the shortness of time, and of its increasing value as we near the terminus of life.

THE CHRISTIAN'S ATTITUDE TOWARD DEATH.

By Prof. Benjamin B. Warfield, D.D., LL.D.

" *For we know that if the earthly house of our tabernacle be dissolved, we have a building from God, a house not made with hands, eternal in the heavens. For verily in this we groan, longing to be clothed upon with our habitation which is from heaven : if so be that being clothed we shall not be found naked. For indeed, we that are in this tabernacle do groan, being burdened : not for that we would be unclothed, but that we would be clothed upon, that what is mortal may be swallowed up in life. Now he that wrought us for this very thing is God, who gave unto us the earnest of the Spirit. Being therefore always of good courage, and knowing that, whilst we are at home in the body, we are absent from the Lord (for we walk by faith, not by sight): we are of good courage, I say, and are willing rather to be absent from the body, and to be at home with the Lord. Wherefore also we make it our aim, whether at home or absent, to be well-pleasing unto him. For we must all be made manifest before the judgment seat of Christ; that each one may receive the things done in the body, according to what he hath done, whether it be good or bad.*"—2 Cor. 5 : 1-10.

NOWHERE more fully than in the opening chapters of the Second Epistle to the Corinthians does Paul describe the trials and distresses of the life that he was living as ambassador of Christ. He had been lately thrown to the beasts at Ephesus, and had escaped, almost miraculously as we may well believe, with bare life. While recovering, perhaps slowly, from the deadly injuries thus received, the news reached him of the threatening defection of the churches of Galatia, and of the danger of that in Corinth, and added mental to his physical distress. For the good of his children in the Lord he controlled the expression of his sorrows, and sent to each of these churches a letter of admonition and instruction, only venturing in that to the Galatians on the pathetic appeal which consisted in calling their attention to the large, misshapen, and painfully formed characters in which alone he could now scrawl the accustomed line or two which he added with his own hand at the end of his letters. Meanwhile things came once more to a climax at Ephesus. Under the leadership of one Demetrius, the craftsmen who made profit out of the service of Diana raised a tumult against the Apostle's preaching; and assembling in the theater, "all with one voice about the space of two hours cried out, 'Great is Diana of the Ephesians!'"— not the first instance in history, nor likely to be the last, when volume and continuance of sound are made to do duty for argument.

Warned by this that the public mind in Ephesus was no longer in a condition to profit by his preaching, Paul departs for Macedonia, apparently before the time appointed for the return of his messengers from Corinth, hoping to meet them on the road. But Titus does not come even at Troas (2 Cor. 2: 13); and torn with anxiety the Apostle pushes on into Macedonia. There at length his returning messengers meet him, and, better than that, bring him good news. The Corinthians allow his authority, and have humbled themselves to his rebukes; and that beloved church at least has ridden safely over the crest of the wave that threatened to submerge it. The burdened heart of the Apostle overflows, and he writes to the Corinthians out of his very soul. For once we see within him, and learn how the stupendous trials which pressed upon him affected his thought and feelings.

Amid all these sufferings, the mere allusions to which, lightly touched as they are, appall us, he is upheld by his sense of the greatness of his work and of the greatness of his hope. Though his outward man is being literally worn away, he need not faint; for his inward man is being renewed day by day, and all this affliction, terrible as it is, is light compared with the eternal weight of glory which it is working for him. His courage draws its force, thus, from his confidence in his future reward. It is because he looks not at the things that are seen, which are temporal, but at those that are not seen, which are eternal, that he can bear all things. Like Moses, he looks unto the recompense of reward, and endures as seeing the Invisible One. Like Abraham, he is content to dwell in tents for a season, because he looks for the city which hath the foundations, whose builder and maker is God. It is, indeed, with just this last figure that the Apostle expresses his feeling here. The reason of his strength, he tells us, is because " we know that if our earthly tent-dwelling be destroyed, we have a house from God, a dwelling not made with hands, eternal, in the heavens." What are earthly sufferings to one who looks upon his very bodily frame as but a tent, in which he sojourns for a time, and expects the laying of it aside to be merely a step toward entering into a mansion prepared for him by God himself?

The Apostle then contemplates the wearing away of his present body with patience. But we must observe that it is not exactly death that he longs for. He is burdened here, and sighs for relief from the burdens of this life, that somehow mortality may be swallowed up by life. But he shrinks from death. He could wish to be alive to greet the Lord when he comes, and so put on the habitation which is from heaven over this earthly tent, rather than be found naked on the coming of that glad day. Not that he expects to live until the Advent; he only could find it in his heart to wish it; he is in entire uncertainty as to the issue, and accordingly adds, "That is, of course, if, when we do put on" (or "when the putting-on time comes") "we shall be found not naked." How instructive meanwhile it is to observe this great soldier of the cross, who was "in deaths oft" and "died daily," shrinking with purely human feeling from the act of death; how magnificent must have been his courage, a courage rooted in nothing human, but in a divine faith and hope. For scarcely has this cry of human nature escaped from him before he proceeds, as if quietly reasoning with himself, to declare that God has wrought us for the very purpose of swallowing up our mortality in life, and given us even here his Spirit as earnest of his intention. And his contemplation being thus withdrawn from self and cast on God, his shrinking from death disappears too. "Being, then, of good courage always," he declares, "and knowing that while we are at home in the body we are away from home from the Lord (for it is by faith that we are walking, not by appearance), we are of good courage, I say, and are well pleased rather to go away from home from the body and go home to the Lord." Thus faith conquers the natural fear of death. As much as he fears it, he longs for the Lord more, and the most direct path that leads to his side, however painful or even unnatural it may be, he will joyfully take.

Paul's whole heart is now before us. He is burdened in this life and longs to be with his Lord. He could wish that the Lord would hasten his coming, and thus "clothe him upon" with immortality; but if this is not to be he earnestly desires even in nakedness of soul to be with him, and welcomes the fearful and unnatural portal of death as access to him. It is the model of the Christian's attitude toward life and death and the life that lies beyond death. Let us seek to make it such for our bruised hearts to-day,* and endeavor to understand from the Apostle's uncovered soul what should be the attitude of our souls toward these great mysteries.

I. First of all, then, we may learn that this life which we are living here cannot be a satisfactory living to a Christian. "In this tent-dwelling," says Paul, "we groan, longing to be clothed upon with our habitation which is from heaven." "We that are in the tent," he repeats, " groan, being burdened,

---

* This sermon was preached on January 17, 1892, the first Sabbath after the death of Prof. Charles Augustus Aiken, Ph.D., D.D.

with a view to the swallowing up of mortality in life." And lest we should think this a state of mind peculiar to himself, as one "in labors more abundant," let us remind ourselves that he elsewhere represents it as characteristic of Christians, broadly declaring that they " who have the first-fruits of the Spirit, even we ourselves, groan within ourselves, waiting for our adoption, to wit, the redemption of our body." This is indeed the whole drift of that great chapter, the seventh of Romans, in which the conflict of the Christian life, that ineradicable strife between the implanted good and the natural evil within us, is vividly portrayed, ending with the heart-rending cry, "O wretched man that I am! who shall deliver me out of this body of death?" It is a body of humiliation, as the Apostle elsewhere calls it, a body of death, a body of sin, with which our spirits are now clothed. How can we fail to long for deliverance from it?

One of the characteristics of the true Christian attitude, then, is that we should be dissatisfied with the life which we are now living in the flesh. This is, of course, not inconsistent with the contentment which is equally a mark of the Christian attitude. The contentment with his lot which the follower of Jesus is called upon to feel and to exhibit, is, at bottom, contentment with Christ and his provision for us, with God and his providential direction of us; so that whatever our Father in heaven sends us we are well content to receive, and whatever hardness he desires us to experience we are glad for his sake to endure. Paul longed to be delivered from this body of death, but he was no stranger to a Christian's content. Years after this he writes to the Philippians that he still cherished his "desire to depart and be with Christ," yet since living in the flesh meant fruit of his work and was needful for them, he was glad to forego what for him was "very far better," and abide with them all for their progress and joy in faith. To be content to fill the place which God assigns us and to do the work which our Lord requires of us is quite consistent with the deepest dissatisfaction with our own Christian attainment and the most passionate longing to perfect our course. To speak of consistency here is indeed short of the mark. The very ground of our dissatisfaction with self is, that we are not what Christ would have us be and fall sadly behind filling the place for which God designs us. Just because we are content with him, we cannot be content with ourselves. And just so long as to us "who would do good, evil is present," as, though we "delight in the law of God after the inward man," we "see a different law in our members bringing us into captivity under the law of sin which is in our members," we must cry, "O wretched man that I am! who shall deliver me out of the body of this death?"

It is for us to ask our souls seriously this day whether this is the case with us. The human heart is very subtle; and it may be that some of us who would fain reply with a hasty "yes" may find cause, on consideration, to doubt whether our dissatisfaction is with self or with God—dissatisfaction with the dispensations of his providence, by which some messenger of sickness or sorrow or failure has visited us. In the bitterness of the moment we may feel glad to leave this world of our misery or our shame, not knowing that the long-suffering of God leadeth us to repentance. The truly Christian dissatisfaction is not such. It is with self and the meagerness of our Christian attainment. And it shows itself in an eager desire not so much to depart from the world as to depart from sin and to sit down in the heavenly places with Christ.

II. We cannot help observing, as a second important truth which we may learn from this unique record of Paul's inner experience, that even to the Christian death remains an undesired guest. Although the Apostle groaned under the burden of his body of sin, and therefore eagerly wished to pass out of this bodily life, yet he expresses a strong desire not to die. He longed rather for the coming of his Lord, that he might go to him without dying. He shrank from death; and it cannot be wrong for other Christians like him to shrink from death. We learn from this at once that though this bodily life which we are now living in the flesh is an evil, and every truly Christian soul will long to be delivered from it, a bodily life in itself considered is not an evil, but a good, and every rightly constituted man must cling instinctively to it. Death is unnatural and rightly terrifies its victims. Even more —death is evil, sin's offspring, Christ's enemy, Satan's servant; and every Christian heart must stand aghast before it. It is only because our Lord and Saviour lies now behind death that we can tolerate the thought of it. To whom of us has this dread presence not come to snatch from our arms one we loved better than life? It has been our comfort and joy that we were surrendering him to the even more loving arms of our Saviour. Since Christ has died, how much of the terror of death has departed! He has broken its sting, which is sin, by removing its strength, which is the curse of the broken law. Since he has lain in it, how much of the gloom of the tomb has gone! But have we not needed all this comfort which we could gain?

The gloom of the tomb still overhangs it; it must, it ought to do so. And terrible death remains terrible still; it bears on its front still the dreadful legend which marks it as God's threatened punishment of sin.

III. In its closest analysis, the horror which we have of death turns on the unnatural separation which it brings about between those life-long companions, the soul and the body. And this leads us to the third great truth which is here brought before us. It is plain that the state of the blessed dead between death and the resurrection, when considered in itself alone as a condition—apart from their case, circumstances, and situation—is an undesirable state, because a state of unnatural separation between soul and body induced by and the fruit of sin. We are apt to think more of the body bereft of its animating and informing principle: even the bodies of our beloved are dear to us. But it is observable that Paul's solicitude seems to be less for the deserted body than for the naked soul. It is its unnatural and sin-born nakedness at death which appalls him; and in this unclothing of the soul he finds the horror of death.

In this sense the state of the blessed dead while awaiting the resurrection, as it is not their final state, is an imperfect state and therefore an undesirable state. In no other sense, however. It is a state of entire happiness; the soul is with the Lord. It is a state of, so far as the soul is concerned, completed salvation, finished sanctification, entire holiness. The Romish invention of purgatory, by which for the great majority of the saved a period of purification of longer or shorter duration and of greater or less suffering is interposed between death and "the going home to the Lord," is not only a baseless but a wicked invention, at war with every statement of Scripture in the premises, and with every dictate of the truly Christian consciousness alike. The same is true, of course, of all the fancies of the so-called ethical theology of our day which agree in supposing the saved soul to carry remainders of sin with it into the other world, because in its subtle and often only half-conscious antagonism to the supernatural this school of thought finds difficulty in believing that God cleanses the soul at death from its remaining sin, according to his Word; and looks only for a self-cleansing by the soul itself in its own activity, which of course would be, however aided by the Spirit, gradual and slow. It is not only the Westminster Confession, but also the Scripture, which teaches in every form of language, and with every circumstance of emphasis possible, that "the souls of the righteous are at their death made perfect in holiness, and are received into the highest heavens, where they behold the face of God in light and glory, waiting for the full redemption of their bodies."

The sole element of truth in the teachings just adverted to lies in the one fact that redemption is incomplete until the resurrection. It is the soul alone which is immediately transferred into holy bliss. The body lies moldering in the grave; and though "even in death," in the beautiful language of the Westminster Larger Catechism, the bodies of Christ's members "continue united to Christ, and rest in their graves *as in their beds,* till at the last day they be again united to their souls," their redemption is not "full" until the resurrection. The salvation is complete, but it is as yet only an incomplete man that is saved. As the separation between soul and body is not natural to man, as God made man's nature, but is the fruit of sin and the penalty specifically threatened to sin, the work of redemption is not "full" until Christ conquers his last enemy, Death, and comes again in triumph, reuniting the souls and bodies of all his saints.

It is not, indeed, a pleasant thought that Christ's enemy, dreadful Death, retains dominion over even this lower element in our nature after death and on through what may well prove to be countless ages, until the Lord comes again in the epiphany of his glory, and in visible conquest over the last of his foes. Do we wonder, in view of such a fact, that the Old Testament saints, in the comparative twilight of revelation, sitting, if not in darkness, yet not yet in the full illumination of the day of salvation, could scarcely speak of death without a shudder, or of the land beyond death except as "a land of darkness and the shadow of death"? Or do we wonder that in the fullness of New Testament light the apostles teach us to long rather for Christ's coming than for death, to wait for that rather than for this, with expectant patience indeed, but also with strong desire? Have we not, indeed, uncovered here the one secret of the gloom that hangs over the Old Testament allusions to the other world, and as well, of that strong emphasis that is placed in the New Testament on the Second Advent which has puzzled many, and which, being misunderstood, has given birth to much Chiliastic error? It was important in the period of preparation that men's minds should not escape from the conception of death as the penalty of sin; and only when life and immortality were ready to be brought fully to light was it safe to make them fully understand the bliss that lay behind death. And now, when preparation has passed into the glorious reality of a completed sacrifice for sin, it is equally important that we should keep in mind that we do not obtain our entire salvation, that all the terrible harvest which springs from sin is not fully garnered by any one of us, until our enraptured eyes behold him who is the Redeemer from sin descending from heaven in like manner as he went into heaven. We are still reaping fruitage from our sin, even after we go abroad from the body and go home to the Lord, or, better, just because in order to go home to the Lord we must needs go abroad from the body.

Let us praise God that he saves the soul at once utterly; and, naked as it may be, takes it home to himself and grants it continual fruition of his favor, while it awaits in his sheltering arms the perfecting of its old companion the body. How great a mercy that our Lord enables us to know that our dead are perfectly holy and happy at once, and that it is only the insensate body that awaits in the disgrace of the tomb the great day when he shall come to be glorified in all his saints. But it is equally important to keep ourselves reminded that they gravely err who speak with scant respect of the body which has also in its measure been a habitation of the Spirit, and is also joined to the Lord, referring to the soul as released from a prison when it is freed from what they are pleased to term the clog of clay. We cannot emphasize too strongly that human souls were not created to exist apart from matter, and so far from needing to be separated from their bodies for their completest freedom, are incomplete and naked things away from their dwelling-houses of clay. It is the glory of Christianity to provide a salvation adequate to the whole man; and though it be only gradually realized, and the soul be taken to bliss long before the renewed and glorified body is prepared for it, yet it is accomplished in the end, and the complete man stands before his God, justified, sanctified, glorified. The saints of God have prelibations of their glory. Even in this world they are received into the number of his sons, and are made temples of the Holy Ghost. When their period of service below is accomplished, their spirits are cleansed from remainders of sin and received into the presence of God. But the day that marks the beginning of their heavenly perfection and of their completed bliss is not the day in which they believed, although in that act their whole salvation was in principle involved; nor yet is it the day in which they depart to be with Christ, although in that they enter into glory; but it is to be the day of Christ's glorious coming and of the resurrection of the saints. And this is the reason of the emphasis on the Day of Judgment in the Bible; it is the day in which the inheritance, incorruptible and undefiled, and that fadeth not away, reserved in heaven for Christ's people, shall be fully revealed.

IV. It is time that we were throwing stress, however, on a further blessed truth brought to us by this passage, and indeed underlying it as one of its foundations; and that is that this intermediate state of the blessed dead, although imperfect when compared with their final state, when the whole man shall partake of the divine glory, is, apart from that comparison, unspeakably blissful, and to be infinitely desired and longed for by every Christian soul. We remember that Paul, with a clear sense of all the unnaturalness of a separation of the soul from the body, yet wished rather to be absent from the body and to be at home with the Lord, and declared to depart and be with Christ to be "very far better." Just so soon as he remembered that while we are at home in the body we are absent from the Lord, he desired to go away from home from the body that he might go home to the Lord. Perhaps no clearer insight could be given of the infinite bliss of the saved soul in heaven than is afforded by the fact that it is so great as to make it intensely to be desired even at the expense of so unnatural a mutilation. Paul does not conceal from his readers that he would rather, for himself, that the coming of Christ should be hastened, so that the conquest of Death, the last enemy, might be completed, and he be glorified, soul and body, without death. But presence with the Lord was so to be yearned for, that, if this was not to be, he was well pleased to depart from the body itself and go to the Lord. It is well to let our hearts dwell on this revelation of bliss. What comfort it brings us for those who have died in the Lord! And perhaps it may entice our own hearts to long to lay aside our body of sin and enter into the inheritance of the saints beyond the grave.

Let us note the superiority of their state to ours here. The evil of our present life is positive evil; all that can be called an evil in the soul-life in heaven is negative only. By which it is intended to say that the holiness and bliss of the disembodied soul in heaven is perfect of its kind; it has only not yet been made a sharer in so complete a glorification of human nature as is destined for it. While, on the other hand, in this life not only do we lag behind the positive attainment there and thus live on a lower plane, but there is a weight of positive evil upon us, a law of sin reigning in our members. Ah, if we could only catch a glimpse of what perfect holiness really is, how would we long to be separated from this body of sin and enter into it at any cost! We observe, therefore, that though the separation of soul and body is in itself an unnatural thing, the separation of our redeemed and sanctifying soul from this body of humiliation in which we now live is a thing to be greatly desired, not because it is a body, but because it is a body of sin. The bliss of the intermediate state is thus infinitely more to be desired than anything that can come to us on earth; it is only less desirable than the completed redemption which is yet to come.

And of this complete redemption it is the earnest and pledge. It is the completion of the salvation of the higher element of our nature, and bears in itself the prophecy and promise of the completion of the salvation of the whole man. It is to be desired, then, as the storm-tossed mariner desires the haven which his vessel has long sought to win through the tossing waves and adverse winds—gate only though it be of the country which he calls home, and long though he may need to wait until all his goods are landed. It is the end of the journey, when the friends come out to meet us. It is within the Father's house, where the greeting rings, "Bring forth the best robe and put it on him." Should the prodigal be impatient for the coming of the robe? The bliss of the holy, happy dwelling with the Lord is such that even were there nothing beyond we should joyfully seek it; and it is the promise and the surety of a yet grander future.

But the Apostle throws his emphasis on the chief joy of the intermediate state. Christ is there. To go abroad from the body is to go home to the Lord. No wonder he prefers nakedness of soul with Christ to personal completeness away from Christ. And no wonder since his day many a bed of suffering has been smoothed, and many a soul has gone forth brightening the face of even the deserted body with its smile of joy as it hears the words of its Saviour, "To-day thou shalt be with me in Paradise." No wonder Christian song is vocal with the sigh

> "O mother dear, Jerusalem!
>   When shall I come to thee?
> When shall my sorrows have an end,
>   Thy joys when shall I see?
> O happy harbor of God's saints,
>   O sweet and pleasant soil,
> In thee no sorrows can be found,
>   No grief, no care, no toil!

> "Jerusalem the city is
>   Of God our King alone;
> The Lamb of God, the light thereof,
>   Sits there upon his throne.
> Ah, God! that I Jerusalem
>   With speed may go and see,—
> Jerusalem! Jerusalem!
>   Would God I were in thee!"

V. Do we not share these yearnings? May God grant that in his own good time each of us may indeed be permitted to join the innumerable throng of praising saints about his throne. Dare we confront the possibility that it may not be so? The Apostle seems to confront it. For, on reaching this point in his statement, he makes a sudden and strange transition. He had reached the climax: "We are of good courage, I say, and are well pleased rather to go away from home from the body, and go home to the Lord." Here he might be expected to pause. But he continues; and the words which he adds demand our serious attention: "*Wherefore also we make it our aim, whether at home or away from home, to be well-pleasing unto him. For we must all be made manifest before the judgment seat of Christ, that each one may receive the things done in the body, according to what he hath done, whether it be good or bad.*" Thus he turns from the glories of his inheritance in Christ in heaven to the duties which he owes him on earth; from the consideration of what he may attain in him to the danger of losing it all; from the bliss of dwelling with Christ to the dread of standing before his judgment-seat. His purpose is obvious, and the addition of these solemn words ceases to be strange. It is not enough to contemplate the glories of heaven; we must seek to make those glories ours. They are given to whom they justly belong; we must all stand before the judgment-seat of Christ and receive according to the deeds done in the body, whether good or bad. And note the finality of this judgment. The Apostle plainly does not contemplate the possibility of any reversal or of any change; the verdict upon what is done here is the irreversible doom of all the future. And therefore it behoves us to be well-pleasing to him.

Oh, the troops upon troops that have laid aside the trials and labors of earth, well-pleasing to their Lord, and entered into their rest with him!

> "Death's wings beat round about us day and night;
> Their wind is on our faces now."

While yet our farewell to them on this side of the separating gulf was sounding in their ears, the glad "Hail!" of their Lord was welcoming them there. May God grant to each of us to follow them. May he give us his Holy Spirit to sanctify us wholly and enable us when we close our eyes in our long sleep to open them at once, not in terrified pain in torment, but in the soft, sweet light of Paradise, safe in the arms of Jesus!

THE VISION OF THE KING IN HIS HOLINESS.

BY PROF. JOHN D. DAVIS, PH.D.

"Then said I, Woe is me! for I am undone; because I am a man of unclean lips, and I dwell in the midst of a people of unclean lips: for mine eyes have seen the King, the Lord of hosts. Then flew one of the seraphim unto me, having a live coal in his hand, which he had taken with the tongs from off the altar: and he touched my mouth with it and said, Lo, this hath touched thy lips; and thine iniquity is taken away, and thy sin purged."—ISAIAH 6:.5–7.

THE event which this chapter records is a vision seen by Isaiah the prophet. The visions of the prophets were, for the most part, private; they were apprehended by the individual, not by his companions. A natural cause sometimes coöperated in producing the vision; the vision of the great sheet let down from heaven, which Peter saw, and the voice heard saying, "Arise, Peter, slay and eat," stood in some relation to his bodily hunger, as the account in the Book of Acts clearly intimates. Thus far have the visions of the prophets points in common with visions begotten of an abnormal mental condition, and to this extent the biblical visions are to be classed as mental phenomena. These facts are only additional proofs of what we should expect, namely, that God, in holding communication with men, worked in accordance with the laws of man's mind.

The visions of the prophets, however, form a unique class. With perhaps one exception, they were granted to holy men only, men who were surrendered to God's service, men between whom and their divine sovereign there had "arisen an understanding." These visions were clearly distinguished by those who saw them from ordinary visions and were recognized as proceeding from God. The visions of the prophets were cautiously accepted by the Church; by law they were not received as genuine until their teaching and their credentials had been subjected to tests. The biblical visions stand alone in the history of religions for purity and righteousness; they were never vain, never meaningless vagaries or lying wonders, but always have a clearly discernible moral and didactic content; and they were often predictive, upon which fulfillment has set the seal of truth. Biblical visions, finally, belong to an age of revelation, and came to men who in manifold manner proved themselves to be vehicles of revelation from God.

This vision which Isaiah saw is in itself simple, but it revolutionized the man. It brought familiar truths into strong relief, focused them on his soul, and burned them into the depths of his nature. It wrought his conversion, or rather, if this chapter is in its proper place, as there is no sufficient reason to deny, it produced what we are wont to call a second conversion: it made God known to him as never before; it brought to light his own true condition by nature; it led him to offer himself for any mission which God might choose. And it was also a revelation: it announced to him an appointed work and disclosed to him the scanty success which should attend his labors for Israel, yea, the hardening of heart and sealing of the eyes of the many which his preaching would produce.

Isaiah in vision saw the King, the Lord of hosts. Host means army, and the title "Lord of hosts" has been supposed to describe Jehovah as God of the armies of Israel. The children of Israel were called God's hosts (Ex. 7:4), and they recognized Jehovah as "the Lord strong and mighty, the Lord mighty in battle." But while the epithet was often applied to Jehovah when he fought for Israel, it was not his official designation as leader of Israel's armies. The word hosts in this connection did not refer to Israelitish troops, but to the armies of the

THE VISION OF THE KING IN HIS HOLINESS. 341

universe, in its spiritual and material aspects, as forming a vast army, in numerous divisions, of various kinds of troops, in orderly array under the command of Jehovah. The Lord of hosts is, as in this vision, the King whose glory fills the universe.

One mighty host in that army consists of the angels. It was the Lord, the God of hosts, which appeared to Jacob at Bethel when he beheld the ladder and the angels of God ascending and descending (Hosea 12: 4, 5); and God's host encamped about him after he separated from Laban (Gen. 32: 2). Their horses and chariots of fire filled the mountain round about Elisha (2 Kings 6: 16). The chariots of God are twenty thousand, thousands of angels (Ps. 68: 17); his messengers who minister unto him and do his pleasure. "Who *in the skies* can be compared unto the Lord? Who *among the sons of the mighty* is like unto the Lord, a God very terrible in the council of the holy ones, and to be feared above all them that are round about him? O Lord God of hosts, who is a mighty one like unto thee, O Jah?" (Ps. 89: 6–8.) Beautifully fitting was it that when Jehovah took upon himself the nature of man and lay as a babe in Bethlehem, a multitude of the heavenly host appeared to celebrate his birth (Luke 2: 13).

Another division of the army under Jehovah's command consists of the stars. The heavenly bodies are repeatedly called the host of heaven On any clear night when we look aloft the aptness of the imagery is apparent. There is no confusion in the starry sky, but order and arrangement. Certain stars are grouped in the form of a bear; others trace the rude outline of a serpent; still others define the magnificent proportions of the mighty hunter. One group forms a cross, another a lyre, another a water-carrier, another a bull, another an eagle. And among them, majestically and without disturbance, move the planets. Truly, "marshaled on the nightly plain, the glittering hosts bestud the sky." The Hebrew people saw the array. Isaiah bids those who would know God to go forth, "lift up their eyes on high and see who hath created these. He who bringeth out [into the field like a general] their host by number, who calleth them all by name," and "upon them layeth commands" (Is. 40:26, 45:12).

Perhaps yet another host was included in the divine title, namely, the forces of nature. They too stand at the bidding of Jehovah. "He sendeth out his commandment upon earth, his word runneth very swiftly;" fire and hail, snow and vapor, not less than stormy wind, fulfill his word. The Lord of hosts sends "the sword, the famine, and the pestilence" (Jer. 29:17). "The Lord, which giveth the sun for a light by day, and the ordinances of the moon and of the stars for a light by night, which stirreth up the sea that the waves thereof roar; the Lord of hosts is his name" (Jer. 31:35).

The Greeks, looking at the heavens above them and at the earth around them, beholding everywhere order, called what they saw cosmos—beauty of harmony. The Romans, discovering the same harmonious relations and movements, named the entirety of creation a universe—combined as one. To the poetic imagination of the Hebrews, with their knowledge of the omnipotent, reigning God, the regularity and order everywhere apparent suggested an army in vast, numerous, and varied divisions acting under the command of one will, and that will Jehovah's. The Lord of hosts, he is the King, the King who sitteth upon the throne of the universe.

Isaiah saw the great King, the Lord of hosts, further, as the Holy One. Seraphim stood before him, crying: "Holy, holy, holy art thou, Lord God Almighty. The whole earth is full of thy glory." It was the glory and making of Israel that the truth of the holiness of God was known and cherished in her borders. When we wander among the nations contemporary with the Hebrews, whether among the kindred peoples in Arabia, or Phœnicia, or the Tigris valley, or farther away among men of another race, among the cultured Greeks, and when we become acquainted with the conceptions of God current among the contemporaneous nations and with the forms of worship in which they engaged, we are amazed to find the truth of the holiness of God shining in its effulgence in the mountains of Judea. Israel alone among the neighboring nations worshiped an absolutely holy God. There was a light in Palestine beyond the brightness of the sun, more beneficent in its influence, powerful to awaken moral life.

The Lord of hosts reveals himself as a moral being even when as King, seated upon his throne, he demands allegiance. He addresses himself to us as our Creator, the former of our bodies, bestower of our faculties, framer of our spirits, and our continual upholder. He addresses himself to us as the possessor of that inherent sovereignty over us which the parent possesses over the young child. On this ground he claims from us obedience, reverence, affection. He is not a usurper; he has erected his throne upon the foundation of truth. Universal sovereignty he claims as a right.

But in another manner God of old revealed his

holiness to Israel: he proclaimed the moral law. In it he laid bare the fact that he cannot be worshiped under the likeness of anything in heaven above or in the earth beneath or in the waters under the earth; for however sublime the object, it is only one of God's thoughts and affords but a partial view of his boundless glory. They that worship God must worship him in spirit and in truth; they must leave his eternal power and moral grandeur in their boundlessness and in their truth.

In the same majestic code God comes before us as he whose name may not be taken in vain. Man bows to power, and fawns upon wealth, and applauds genius; he feels respect for moral worth alone. God appeals to this innate homage to worth. He does not desire unwilling submission, nor to be courted for favors, nor to be given applause; he requires the reverence due unto his name. He discloses his glorious character to our moral judgment: a character which is above vanity; which overawes frivolous mention, awakens the deepest emotions of our being, commands the admiration, reverence, homage, and adoration of our moral nature.

Again does God come before us in the ten commandments, speaking to us now of our relation to our fellow-men, requiring of us a moral life; requiring of thee, O man, that thou do justly, and love mercy, and walk humbly with thy God.

Yet again the Lord comes before us in the precepts of the law and in the reasons annexed thereto "glowing with zeal for all that is pure and good and holy and true, ever engaged in separating the holy and true from the unholy and false, striving to do it first by mercy, and if man makes that fail, then by the cutting off of his judgments"; a God delighting in the presence of holy ones and bountifully blessing them; a God who cannot behold iniquity, the awful outflow of whose indignation is against sin, but against sin only—a fire consuming iniquity.

These were the familiar thoughts which were brought home to Isaiah. He saw God in a single vision as the King of the universe and the absolutely Holy One. At the sight he cried out, "Woe is me! for I am undone; for I a man of unclean lips . . . have seen the King, the Lord of hosts." There was a widespread belief in Israel that no man could see God and live. The cry of Isaiah did not spring from intellectual assent to that doctrine; it was the soul's realization of the fact.

In contrast with the King, Isaiah saw himself a rebel. In the presence of God, man must see himself thus. In our souls we know two things. We know that if God exists, he is our King. We cannot away with that. We can mock, we can stifle the voice of nature in us, we can stop our ears; and yet when all things stand naked and revealed we are forced to confess that he is our lawful King. We know also that we have rebelled against him; we know that we have gone stubbornly every one his own ways. Upon this fundamental thought the writers of Scripture dwell—that before the secret tribunal of man's most inmost soul, sooner or later, willing or unwilling, man must confess the truth that God is his lawful sovereign. And with that confession must come from him who has not obeyed the truth the cry, "Woe is me! for I am undone; for I have seen the King, the Lord of hosts." No place for me in the kingdom of God. Banishment is my lot. I know the condemnation of the King—not spoken in words alone, of which the sound will die, not written on perishable parchment, but uttered by the soul: "Depart with everlasting destruction from the presence of the Lord."

But these are not the only floods of conviction which are bound, sooner or later, to rush upon the soul. In the presence of the King, the King of glory, whose nature is holiness, in the presence of that company of holy angels, the prophet saw himself unclean, and the sense of his defilement overwhelmed him. Seraphim, who had never rebelled, never sinned, could surround the throne, could adore, and in overpowering admiration could cry, "Holy, holy, holy art thou, Lord God Almighty"; but his lips, although they had often spoken God's name, were unfit to ascribe holiness to the Holy One. Back of the lips was the heart, and because of the heart he was unable to render the lips as sacrifice.

It is easy for God to show to us our guilt: a vision to Isaiah; an opening of the eyes to our first parents; a thunder-storm witnessing to God's power in nature recalling pious Job to a proper attitude toward God; an earthquake shock at Philippi awakening the jailer to his sinful, lost condition; a still, small voice to Elijah; a parable to David; an overlooked truth to Nicodemus; a glimpse of the past life to the woman at Sychar. Verily it is but a thin veil that hides the sinfulness of our hearts from our eyes, if hidden it be. The breath of God sweeps it away. He needs but to suggest to us, for example, this: Do you ever do what your conscience or the Bible tells you is wrong? Do you ever go your own way and not God's? Do you always bow to the holy law of God as the supreme rule of right, and are you always influenced by a governing regard for God?

And toward your fellow-men do you entertain pure thoughts only, and kindly and chaste and unenvious desires toward your neighbor and your rival? In the words of that wondrous summary, do you love God with all your heart at all times, and your neighbor equally as yourself? Love never faileth. Love seeketh not its own, is not provoked, taketh not account of evil, rejoiceth not in unrighteousness, but rejoiceth with the truth.

Those may ascend God's holy hill who have clean hands and a pure heart. To ascend means to stand in the visible presence of the King; to occupy a place in the circle about the throne; to worship him whose awful indignation against sin is a consuming fire; to be under the gaze of the all-seeing eye which regardeth not the outward appearance, but searcheth the heart; and there venture to cry, "Holy, holy, holy art thou, Lord God Almighty."

In the presence of the King, the Lord of hosts, the Holy One, Isaiah saw himself undone. But when he lost all hope of being able to stand before the holy God he learned that God can save the sinner, that God only can save, and that God saves without the sinner's help. It is the lost whom God finds. It is the soul burdened by the sense of its guilt which God is willing to relieve. Oh, blessed suffering when it is the forerunner of God-given relief! When he discovered himself undone Isaiah saw an altar,—as long afterwards the Apostle John saw, standing amidst the company about the throne, the Lamb as it had been slain from the foundation of the world. It brought to the prophet's mind the familiar teaching of propitiation, of that shedding of blood without which there is no remission of sins; and that the holy God, whose just indignation against sin is the destruction of the sinner, has nevertheless established an altar in the precincts of the palace. He saw a live coal taken from off the altar with tongs by a messenger sent forth by God, and laid upon his lips with the words, "Lo, this hath touched thy lips; and thine iniquity is taken away and thy sin purged." He saw the altar, he heard that it availed for him, and that by God's work he was rendered guiltless in God's sight. He saw the burning coal, and perhaps he discerned in it somewhat of the baptism with the Holy Ghost and with fire, which purifies the soul and makes it fit for the Master's use. God burns out the sin in mercy that the sinner be not consumed in wrath. And lo! the holiness of God has extended the sphere of holiness; it has freed a sinner from guilt; it has kindled a flame in him which will work for righteousness; it has added another to the number of the saints.

It is a matter of common observation that the greatest sinners often make the greatest saints. There is reason for this fact, and in part it is because the great sinner beholds the awful pit in which he was fallen, discerns most profoundly the necessity for and the efficacious power of the sacrifice on Calvary, and apprehends most vividly the wonders of redeeming love. But there is no need that one be a great criminal in order to become a great saint. It is only necessary for any man to obtain a true view of the desperate wickedness of his heart, and at the same time a right conception of the absolute holiness of God, in order to be revolutionized in conversion and to become an unwearied publisher of man's lost condition by nature, and of the free grace of God in Christ. Paul is sometimes falsely cited as the great sinner becoming the great saint. He is really the example of a conscientious, strictly moral though misguided servant of God, transformed by one focused glimpse of the crucified, risen Jesus as Saviour and Lord into the fearless, tireless missionary of the cross and scepter of the Christ. So, too, Isaiah would seem to have been a godly man before the vision; but after the vision, he it is who, more than any other writer of Scripture, dwells upon those attributes of God which are comprehended in the two titles, "Lord of hosts," and "Holy One of Israel"; and if we mistake not, he is the prophet who diligently proclaimed that we all like sheep have gone astray; that all our righteousnesses are as filthy rags; that the holiness of God devours the land in judgment, burning until the cities be left desolate; and he is the prophet who lifts up with greatest urgency to dying Israel and a dying world the suffering, atoning Saviour offering salvation for a look, to every one, without money and without price.

Who wrote the last twenty-seven chapters of the Book of Isaiah? The man who had the vision.

Who is it that became the faithful servant of God, ready for a service of large disappointment and popular dislike? He who saw God as the King, the Lord of hosts, the Holy One, and himself as the rebel, guilty, lost, subject to the justifying grace and sanctifying work of God.

The Lord grant that we, through the written Word and by the work of the Spirit, may likewise apprehend the King in his glory and be revolutionized.